INTRODUCTION TO DRAWING

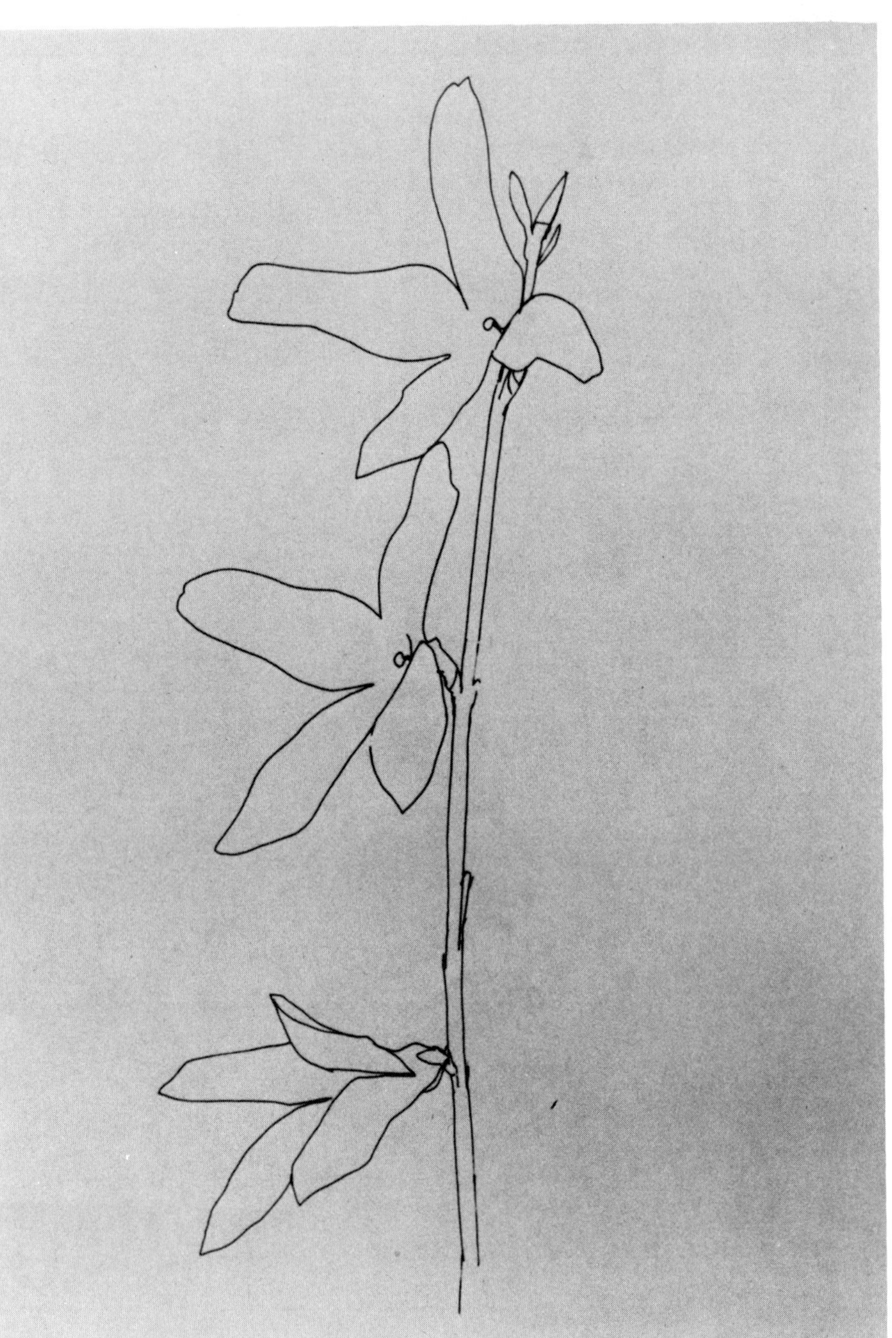

INTRODUCTION TO DRAWING

ROGER WINTER
Southern Methodist University

Prentice-Hall, Inc., Englewood Cliffs, N.J. 07632

Library of Congress Cataloging in Publication Data

Winter, Roger, 1934–
    Introduction to drawing.

    Includes index.
    1. Drawing. I. Title.
NC710.W6   1983   741.2   82-13195
ISBN 0-13-480756-1
ISBN 0-13-480749-9 (pbk.)

Frontispiece. *Forsythia,* by Ellsworth Kelly. 1969. Ink, 29″ ×
23″. Collection of the artist. (Cova-Jakori).

Editorial/production supervision
  and interior design by Virginia Livsey
Cover design by Wanda Lubelska Design
Manufacturing buyer: Ronald Chapman

ISBN 0-13-480756-1
ISBN 0-13-480749-9 (pbk.)

Printed in the United States of America

10 9 8 7 6 5 4 3 2 1

Prentice-Hall International, Inc., *London*
Prentice-Hall of Australia Pty. Limited, *Sydney*
Editora Prentice-Hall do Brazil, Ltda., *Rio de Janero*
Prentice-Hall of Canada Inc., *Toronto*
Prentice-Hall of India Private Limited, *New Delhi*
Prentice-Hall of Japan, Inc., *Tokyo*
Prentice-Hall of Southeast Asia Pte. Ltd., *Singapore*
Whitehall Books Limited, *Wellington, New Zealand*

To Jane Cullen,
for her encouragement and patient help
during the early stages of this book

CONTENTS

Chapter 7   **OUTSIDE SOURCES**   83

Chapter 8   **CRITICISM**   95

Conclusion   105

Index   109

PREFACE

> *Drawing itself is a part of learning: learning to use one's eyes to see more intensely. To encourage everybody to draw is not to turn people into artists, just as you don't teach grammar to turn them all into Shakespeares.*
>
> *Henry Moore*

This book offers an approach to the study of drawing for the general student. It is based on the premise that drawing, as a means to develop the senses, order space, and broaden thought, is a beneficial discipline within everyone's reach, like reading and math.

Some of the ideas in the book are new; others are borrowed from tradition. In either case I try to stay clear of the dogmatic because I doubt that drawing, with all its variations, can be taught from a fixed position. The book's emphasis of the study of objects and models should not be misconstrued to mean that natu-ralism is a favored style. This is a book about underlying visual principles, not styles. The objective world is heavily relied on because it provides a meeting ground where communication between student and teacher and peer and peer is heightened by mutual experience. Through the study of objects, the user of this book not only discovers the power of observation but also makes contact with materials, process, structure, mass, gesture, intuition, and criticism.

The chapters are arranged so that if used sequentially, the reader is presented with a coherent system of study. But whether or not the chapters are approached in order, all the ideas presented must be experienced before the user can expect to gain an intimate, working knowledge of what the verb *to draw* really means. A suggested amount of time to spend with each idea or exercise is always given, but these times are no more than experienced guesses and may often have to give way to personal needs.

Drawings can be anything from preparatory studies to highly finished objects, or something else entirely. To define the *noun* drawing would be to name its every historical shape. Such a definition, even if possible, would not face the real problem of understanding the *verb* drawing. Drawing is a process, a search. The more honest the search, the finer the product will be. Throughout this book, drawing is considered to be a balancing of perception and form. Perception overemphasized leads to mindless rendering. Form-making without the discipline of observation can quickly gravitate to surface decoration in the hands of the inexperienced. A sense of form is at the core of the aesthetic consciousness that gives order to the marks and spaces that make up drawing. The French word for drawing, *dessin*, makes a healthy suggestion that drawing must be more than just copying nature. But good observation brings authority and magic to form.

ACKNOWLEDGMENTS

The expertise and effort of many people went into the making of this book, and I am grateful for all the generous help I received. I especially wish to thank Virginia Livsey for her painstaking care as production editor. I also thank the museums, galleries, private collectors, artists, and others who permitted me to reproduce the works used as illustrations, and the various publishers and writers for their permission to print the quotes used throughout the book. Thanks to the many students and ex-students whose work I have relied upon so heavily as a source of illustrations; the photographers for their valuable help; the people who appear in classroom photographs; those who helped me translate letters, find addresses, and send permission requests; those who critiqued my ideas; and all the others who were supportive and indulgent in so many ways.

R. W.

INTRODUCTION
TO
DRAWING

Chapter 1
MATERIALS

MAKING CONTACT

Before you can make significant breakthroughs in learning to draw, you must first make contact with your materials— make them an extension of yourself. Initiates to drawing (with the exception of young children) often find that they are afraid to touch the black chalks and wet clay with which they are expected to work, and that these inhibitions present the first obstacle in learning to draw. Every year or two, a student will ask me if it's allright to wear rubber gloves to class so materials won't get on his or her skin. Another drawing teacher told me the story of a student who wrapped Kleenex around vine charcoal in order to keep her fingers clean. Fear of getting dirty results from living in a time when cleanliness is worshipped. This fetish is kept alive by advertisers telling us how to clean our clothes, bodies, and houses.

The sense of touch is further inhibited by our having moved irreversibly away from a world where we are expected to make things with our hands. Instead, we push buttons in a world of technological wonders.

It is easy to understand how a newcomer to drawing might feel inhibitions, even revulsion, when first confronted by the greasy, wet, chalky substances with which he or she is supposed to make something. The casual clutter of a typical drawing room after the first hour of class

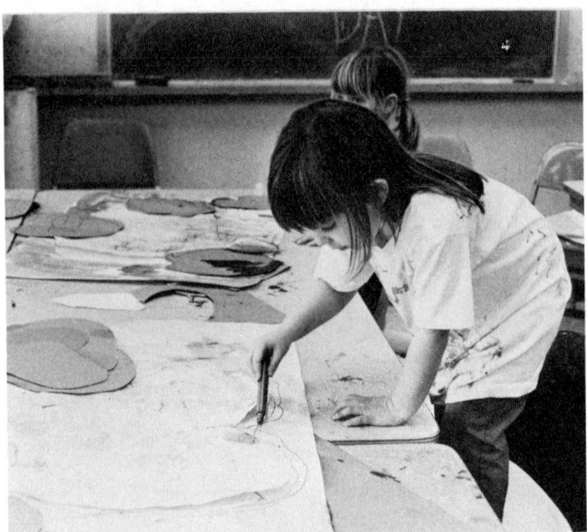

Figure 1-1. You can emulate the curiosity, the fun-seeking nature of a child. (James Flannery).

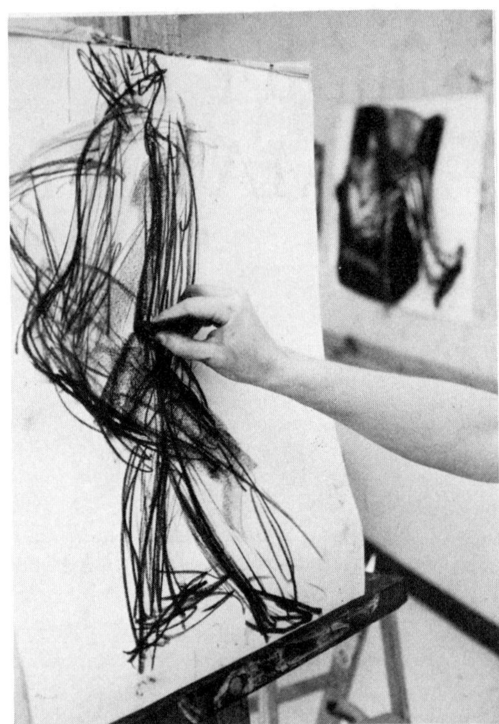

Figure 1-2. Your materials must become an extension of yourself. (Author).

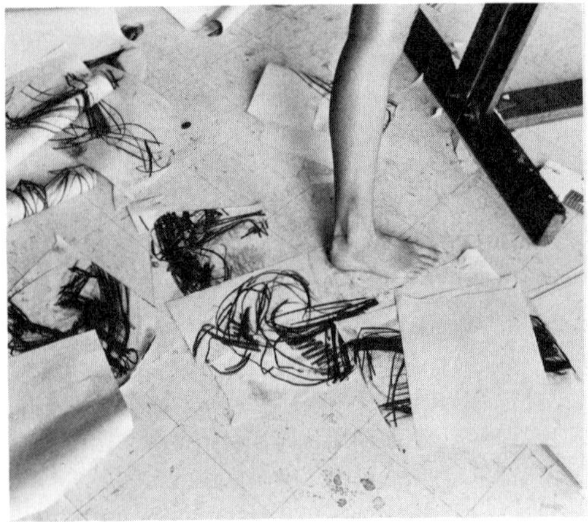

Figure 1-3. The clutter of a typical drawing room looks "messy" to a newcomer. (Author).

(Fig. 1-3), with newsprint and broken chalk scattered around the floor, looks "messy" to anyone not familiar with the leeway a person drawing must have in order to focus full attention on his or her work.

Overcoming negative responses to typical materials and workroom conditions of drawing may be natural and painless. On the other hand, it may require conscious effort. You must first make it clear in your own mind when cleanliness is sensible and when it is unreasonable. Insisting on keeping your hands and clothes spotless in a drawing class is an unreasonable idea, because it inhibits involvement with drawing. Second, consider that drawing, in an automated world, may be one of the last resorts for tactile discovery and hand work. Drawing can be as pleasurable as playing at the beach, and it shares with this activity a harmless rebellion against the excessive neatness of civilized life.

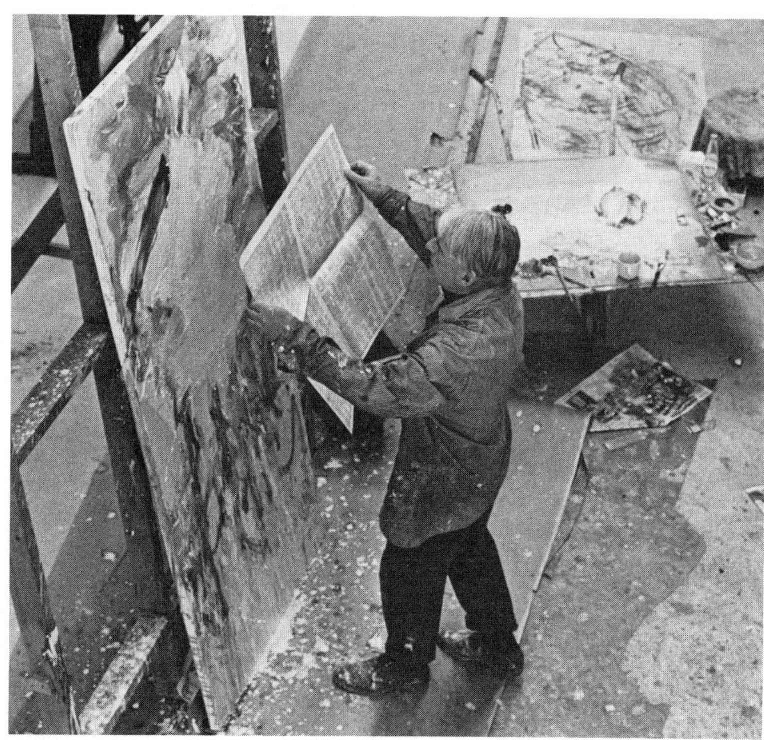

Figure 1-4. Willem de Kooning in Easthampton, 1964. (Hans Namuth).

Your first response to a new material may be to hold it at arm's length and do as little as possible to change its store-bought shape. No one can draw with this attitude, so you must overcome it quickly. Play with a new material for several minutes before moving on to serious drawing with it. For instance, work the sharp edges off the ends and sides of a conté crayon by rubbing it all over a sheet of paper until all of its corners are rounded. This will help you make contact with the material, and it will also make the conté crayon a more sensitive tool by facilitating its movement over the paper.

The first time you confront ink and brush, you should sacrifice a sheet or two of paper by making big fluid drips, splashes, and spatters all over the page, using a big soft brush filled with ink. When I introduce ink to my class, I some-

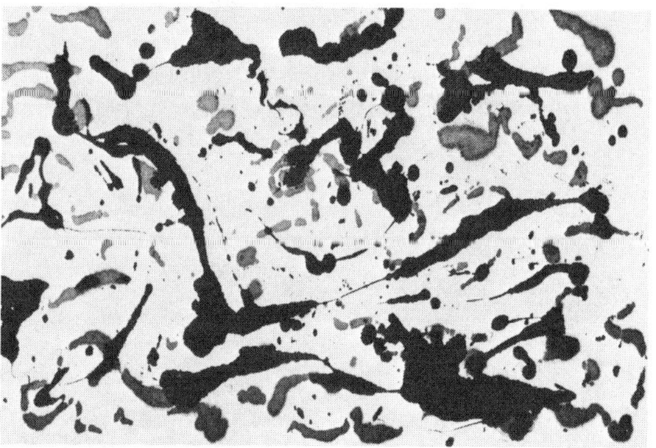

Figure 1-5. Untitled drawing, by Jackson Pollock. 1951. Sepia and black inks on paper, 24⅞″ × 36⅞″. Courtesy of Ms. Lee Krasner Pollock, from *Jackson Pollock: Works on Paper*, by Bernice Rose (Museum of Modern Art, New York, 1969).

times drop an ink-filled brush onto a clean sheet of paper just to let the class see what happens (and also to demonstrate that dropping things or spilling something is not so tragic after all). Remember that you are trying to get the feeling of a *liquid* medium—it is the *flow* you are after.

With clay, you can punch it, pull it, flatten it out, roll it into a ball, break it in half, and push it back together. A young child might go so far as to taste or smell the clay to get at the nature of this strange new material. (I am not suggesting that you or the child should ever taste a material, since some of them are toxic. However, you can emulate the curiosity, the fun-seeking nature of a child).

PREVIEWING MATERIALS AND TOOLS

The best way to learn about an unfamiliar material is to use it in a drawing. Therefore, each of the following materials and tools will be reintroduced at an appropriate time with a correlated drawing approach.

Conté

This dry, hard material is sold in small bar-shaped sticks. Its capacity for a great range of tones makes it appropriate for light and dark studies; its atmospheric quality makes it ideal for drawing masses (see Chapter 5). Conté can be applied directly with the edge of the bar or the end of the bar and then left alone, spread around with the fingers and hands, or smoothed into veils of tone with a chamois cloth (the same material used for drying and polishing cars). The combination of direct and indirect (rubbed and erased) applications of conté resembles the rich tones attained when printmaking methods are mixed. A kneaded eraser is the most effective tool for erasing conté. When a kneaded eraser begins to get dark from use, you can pull, knead, and shape it until you find a clean area of the eraser.

Figure 1-6.   Conté crayon's capacity for a wide range of tones makes it appropriate for light and dark studies. *A Monkey* (*Study for La Grande Jatte*), by Georges Seurat. 1884–85. Conté crayon, 5¼″ × 28½″. Courtesy of Mrs. Henry D. Sharpe. (Museum of Art, Rhode Island School of Design, Providence).

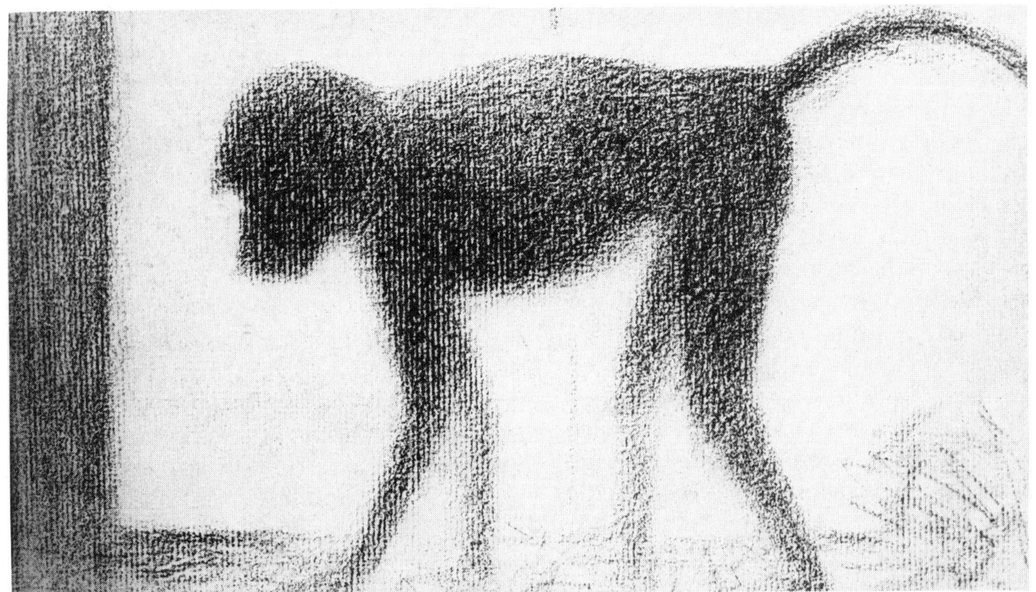

Pencil and Scissors

In the context of this book, pencils are not used for sketching or any other technique popularly associated with this tool (rendering, shading, rubbing, and so on). These methods have been fully explained in various other drawing books, and I feel no need to go into them again. Instead, I recommend that you use pencils, or scissors, for making simple outlines that divide one shape from another. Lines drawn with a pencil or cut with scissors permit no ambiguities (see Figs. 1-7 and 1-8) and are therefore perfect for establishing boundaries. A common No. 2 writing pencil and a pair of utility scissors will suffice for my purposes, although a wide range of hard and soft drawing pencils are sold in the art stores (*H* is the hard range; *B* and *F*, the soft), and special scissors are available for cutting silhouettes. A standard bar eraser, such as a Pink Pearl, is the best one for erasing pencil lines.

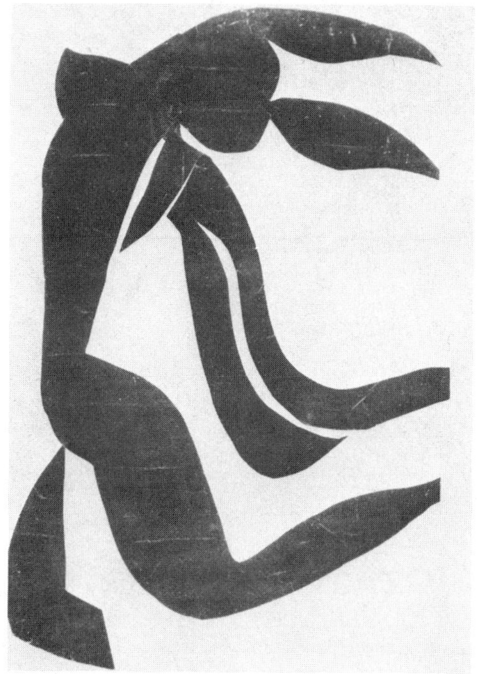

Figure 1-8. Scissor-cut lines permit no ambiguities. *Blue Dancer,* by Henri Matisse. 1952. Blue gouache decoupée with faint traces of charcoal, 42½″ × 31″. Collection of The Baltimore Museum of Art. (Claude Duthuit).

Ink

Fluidity is the essence of ink. You only get into trouble with it when you see its wetness as a flaw and try to turn it into a dry material—suddenly it becomes an unmanageable mess. But if you accept its wetness, its fluid quality, you begin to see that it has a marvelous flow, a life of its own. Let it flow, while offering it a minimum of direction. India ink, the most common drawing ink, is the only kind you'll need to use with this book. However, there are other inks on the market (China, plain writing, ink in various colors), and you should not hesitate to become familiar with these even though they are not specifically recommended. Some materials, such as diluted oil paint

Figure 1-7. Pencil lines divide shape from shape. *Four Oranges,* by Ellsworth Kelly. 1966. Pencil, 22½″ × 28¼″. Collection of The Solomon R. Guggenheim Museum, New York. (Robert E. Mates).

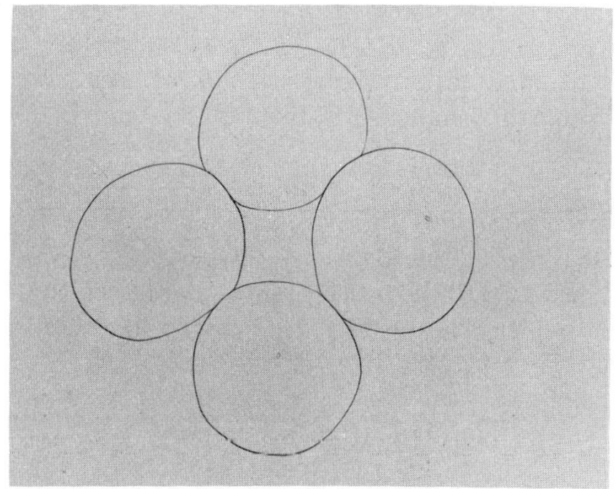

5

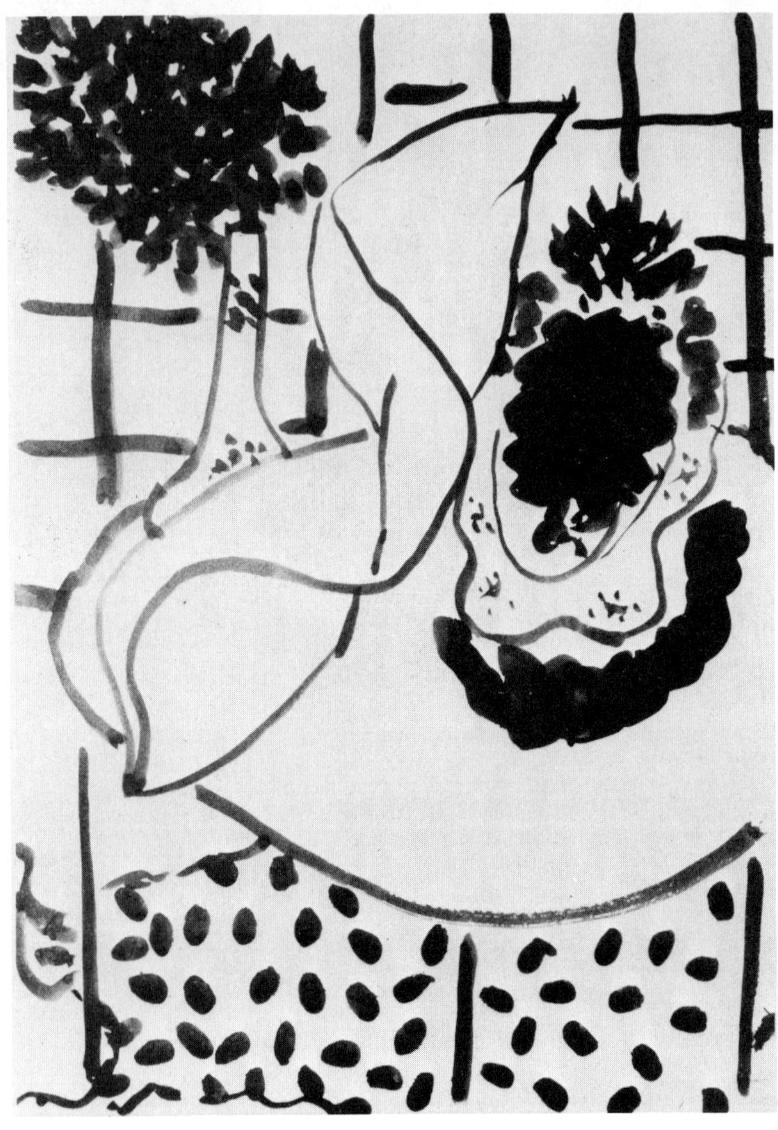

Figure 1-9. *Still Life with Pineapple*, by Henri Matisse. 1948. Brush and ink on white paper, 41″ × 28⅛″. Private collection. (© SPADEM, Paris/VAGA, New York, 1982).

and water color, handle like ink and could be used as an option in the ink exercises.

Brushes

The only brush I suggest is a medium- or large-sized bamboo brush. My description of brush quality invariably refers to such a brush. You should understand that bristle brushes and small or differently shaped sable-type brushes will have quite different qualities. They are not automatic substitutes for the bamboo brush.

The way a brush holds and dispenses liquid gives it a spontaneous, fleeting quality not found in any other conventional tool. If the brush is filled with water and you dip only the tip or one side of the brush into the ink, the resulting stroke can contain a range of lights and darks. Through experimentation, you will get to know when, and in what amounts, to use water for thinning the ink so that a brushstroke will have the desired degree of darkness. A bold, confident brushstroke is a beautiful sight in itself. In contrast, a hesitant, worried stroke is painful to see. A brush makes a particularly inadequate pencil, so you shouldn't try to turn it into one. You should wet its bristles and fill them with ink, hold it out at the end of its handle, and move it across and around the page— welcoming the happy accident.

Clay

Clay is an extraordinarily malleable material, and a very useful material in drawing. Drawing a model from the infinite points of view made possible by clay brings the eyes and the sense of touch into use in ways that drawing a model from one point of view can never do. The formal aims of a clay study, which occupies a volume in the round, are quite different from those of a study

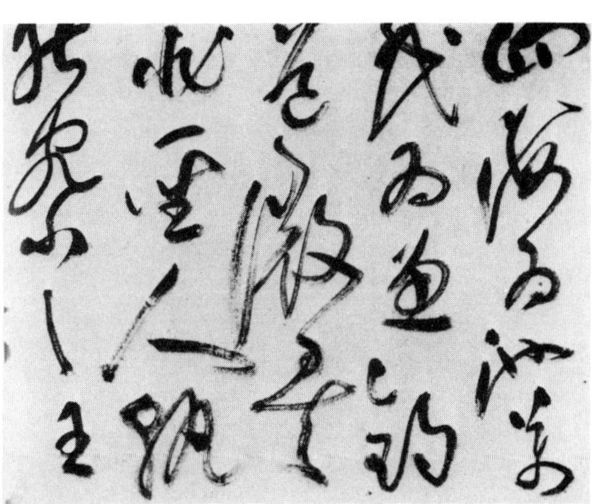

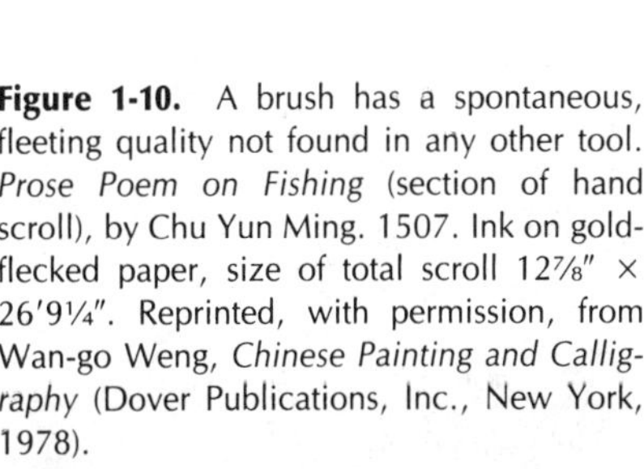

Figure 1-10. A brush has a spontaneous, fleeting quality not found in any other tool. *Prose Poem on Fishing* (section of hand scroll), by Chu Yun Ming. 1507. Ink on gold-flecked paper, size of total scroll 12⅞" × 26'9¼". Reprinted, with permission, from Wan-go Weng, *Chinese Painting and Calligraphy* (Dover Publications, Inc., New York, 1978).

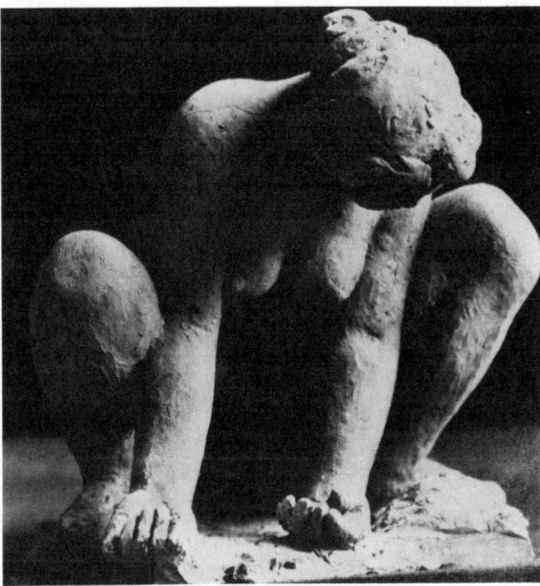

Figure 1-11. Clay brings the sense of touch into use as the model is studied from multiple points of view. *Woman With a Crab* (front view), by Aristide Maillol. 1930. Clay, 6" × 4¾". Courtesy of Galerie Dina Vierny. (© SPADEM, Paris/VAGA, New York, 1982).

done on a two-dimensional page, where the composition must conform to a rectangular plane. Nevertheless, making clay studies from a model is related to drawing—or can be, at least—since it entails perceiving and forming. It is also an unusually sensitizing tactile experience. You will need no tools other than your hands, although a stick with a wire loop on the end of it (called a *sling tool*) is useful in cutting away precise amounts of clay in involved areas of a study.

Collage

Collage has the capacity to produce instant areas of color, and is therefore related to painting more than it is to drawing, in a strictly traditional sense. But collage has its uses in a drawing class as an adventurous, spontaneous method of studying the model or other objects, because it forces us to get into the background spaces. Collage is also a useful medium for making compositional stud-

Figure 1-12. Collage, with its capacity for instant color, facilitates getting into background spaces. *The Woodshed*, by Romare Bearden. 1969. Collage on board, 40½″ × 50½″. (Metropolitan Museum of Art, George A. Hearn Fund, New York).

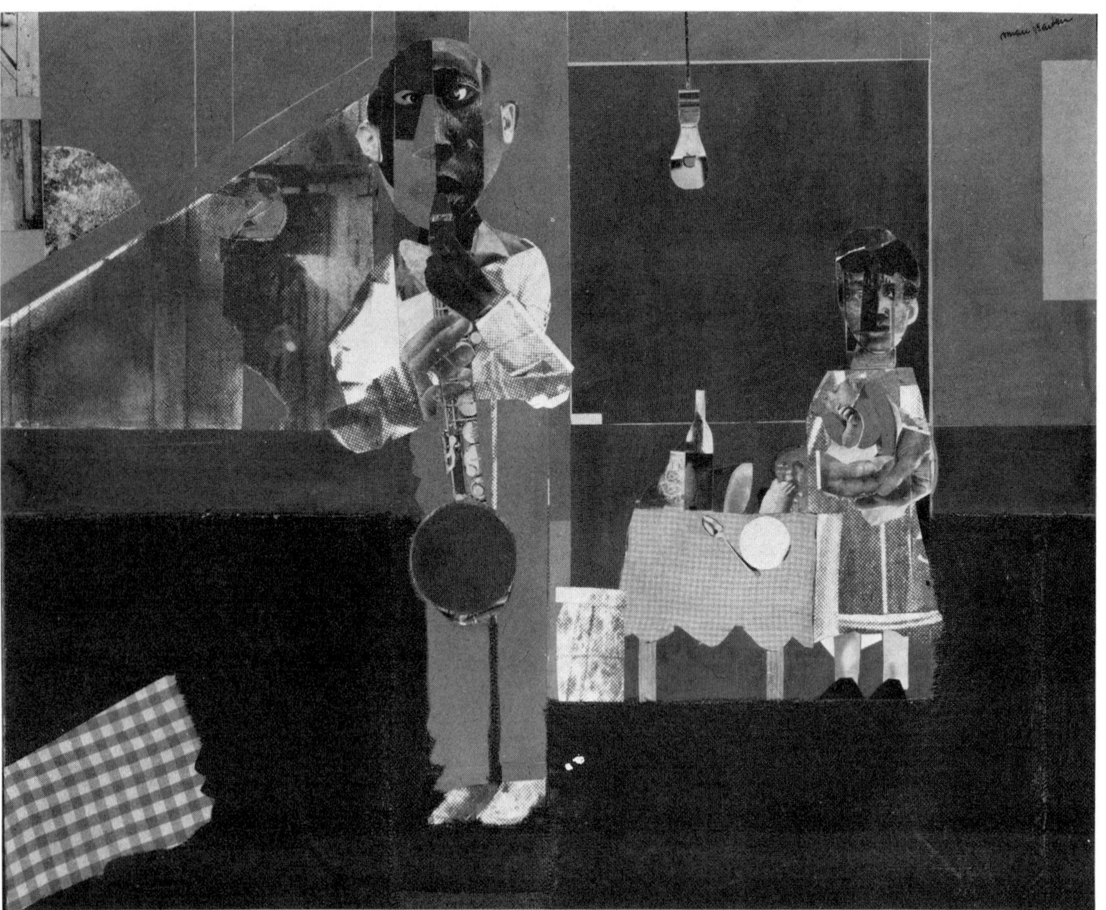

ies of paintings (see Chapter 4). So why not make use of it? I do not insist on the tight media boundaries that some teachers do.

Use colored paper found in magazines, wrapping paper, and all sorts of printed material rather than purchased packets or large sheets of colored paper, as the latter are coldly consistent. In addition to colored paper you will need rubber cement, scissors, and cardboard.

Paper

Most of the work prescribed in this book can be done on rough newsprint paper. Various sizes of newsprint pads (from 9″ × 12″ to 24″ × 36″) are sold in art supply stores. You may be able to buy or have for free the end of a roll of newsprint from a newspaper printing department. Rolls can be cut into desired sizes with a paper cutter or straight edge and mat knife. The soft surface of newsprint will not take too much erasing, and in cases where a thicker, harder paper is needed, I suggest a standard all-purpose pad, such as the Strathmore pads or their equivalent.

SUMMARY

In this chapter I discuss the importance of making contact with materials and the detriment to progress that can come from tactile inhibitions and fear of getting dirty. I suggest steps toward overcoming such inhibitions.

I describe ways of playing with materials before trying to use them in more serious work.

All the materials recommended for use in subsequent chapters are previewed. (I have chosen to omit certain popular materials from this book—pens, chalks, and charcoal—because I think that they are not pertinent to the purpose of the book as stated in the preface. In my experience, pens have proven to be too tight, scratchy, and technique-oriented for beginners; chalk and charcoal, too soft.)

Chapter 2
MEASURING

Proportion (n): 1. The relationship of one part to another or to the whole with respect to magnitude, quantity, or degree: ratio 2. balance, symmetry
Proportion (vt): 1. To adjust (a part or thing) in size relative to other parts or things 2. to make the parts harmonious or symmetrical

from Webster's New Collegiate Dictionary

GETTING STARTED

Your first drawing will be a simple line study of a cube. Before you really start to draw, I submit the following general advice and information with high hopes that it will help you form some good habits and see more clearly right at the beginning.

Always stand at an easel when you draw. Give yourself plenty of room to back up. Stay an arm's length away from your drawing at all times so that you will be aware of the full size of your page and just where you are placing things on the page. You cannot keep an objective atti-tude toward your work if your eyes are right up at the drawing.

Chapter 4 deals extensively with placement, positive-negative relation-ships, and other matters of compositional form. For now, just remember to fill up the page with the object or objects being drawn. Use the greatest amount of page space without leaving anything out.

Be sure to set up your easel so that you can see the object you are drawing *and* the page you are working on without turning your head. All you should have to move are your *eyes*, looking back and forth from the page to the object and the space around it. *If you have to keep turning*

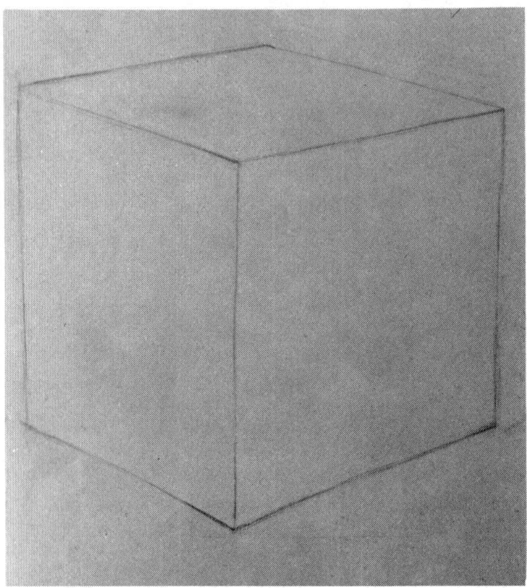

Figure 2-1. Line drawing of a cube, by Marilu Gruben (art education major). (Jean Mitchel).

your head from object to page, you will lose too much information in the turns.

Never be afraid to make needed changes, but avoid the habit of erasing every mark you put down.

In order to get the most value from this chapter, you will need some simple geometric solids. These can be built easily, using pieces of mat board, a mat knife, a straight edge, and white glue. Alternatively, you can build them from materials you have on hand. Cones can be made with heavy paper. Coffee cans covered with white paper make adequate cylinders. Ready-made spheres, such as toy balls, are sufficient. Every form should be white so that the lights and darks stay consistent throughout a setup. The lights and darks you see at this point must come from light phenomena rather than from surfaces painted in different light and dark colors. Pigment variations will only confuse your perception of volume.

No two people will work exactly alike, not even while following the same exercise and instructions. Each person will bring something individual to his or her first effort. Never abandon the purpose of an exercise, however, take note of the personal tendencies in your work and in the works of other students. All your life you have recognized people because of differences in their speech, manners, and looks, and these differences have helped to make life interesting. Now you will learn even more about yourself and other people through looking at drawings. The famous American teacher and painter Robert Henri urged his students to trust their own emotions from the first day of art class. Trusting yourself is a part of drawing, as is the humility needed to study simple solids for the sake of understanding volume in space.

Figure 2-2. Stand at an easel and stay an arm's length away from your drawing. (Lynn Martin).

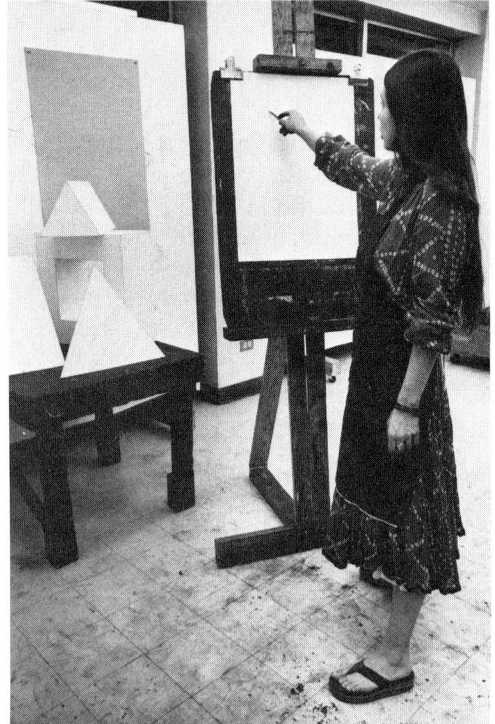

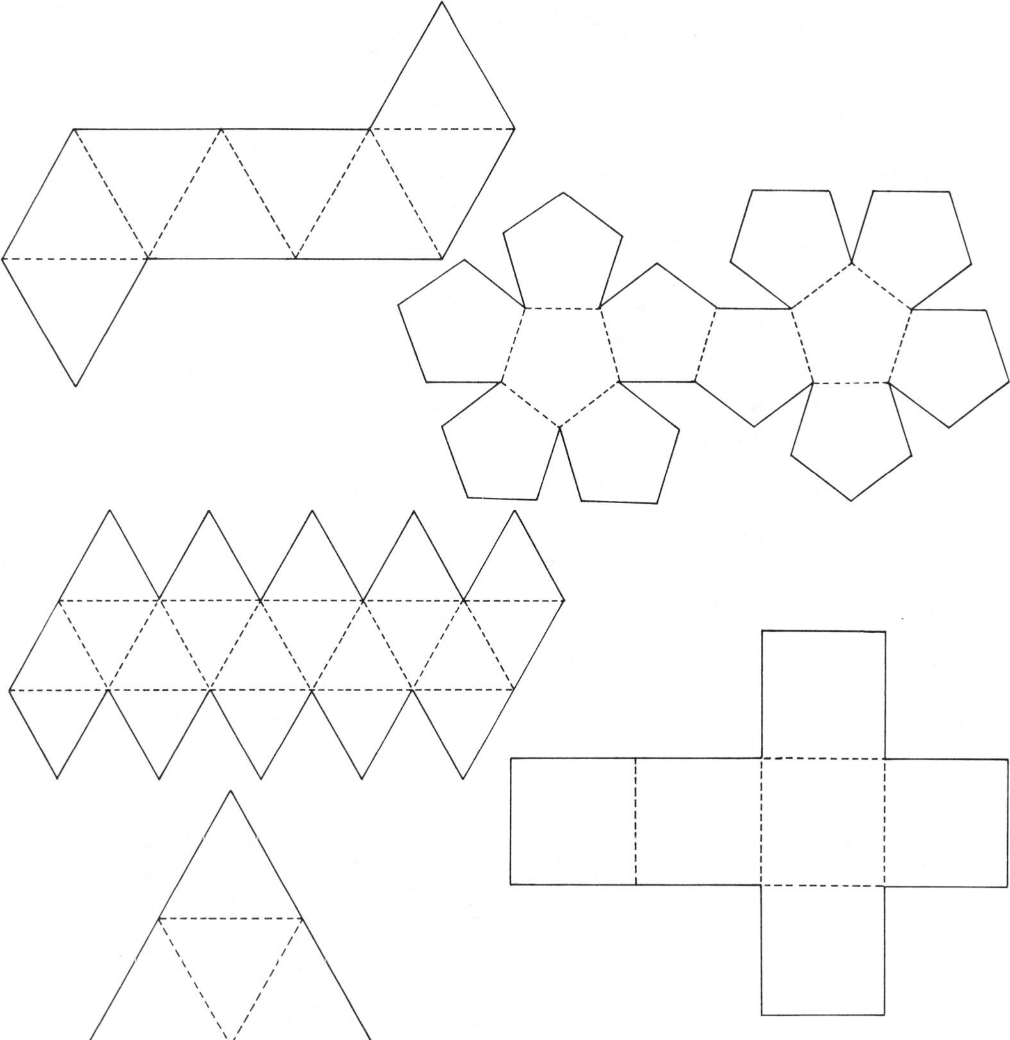

Figure 2-3. Simple geometric solids can be built easily using patterns like these, some mat board, a mat knife, a straight edge, and white glue.

SIZE AND ANGLE

Place a cube on a table so that you can see three of its planes. Clamp a sheet of 18″ × 24″ newsprint paper to a masonite panel or other drawing board. Adjust the easel to accommodate your standing height. Stand with a No. 2 writing pencil (or No. 2B drawing pencil) in your hand. Hold the pencil by the eraser end—don't use a death grip down by the sharpened end. Start to think about how you will fill up the page with the single form of the cube. *Ghost drawing* (moving your hand around the page without making any marks) may be useful. Draw one line, anywhere on the page, which corresponds to a line in the cube. By drawing this one line, you will have built in a ruler by which all other measurements can be taken. Your eyes and hand may work out a finer ruler as the drawing progresses, and you may be forced to abandon the size, angle, and placement of the original line, but let the first line guide you for the moment. Make a conscious effort at drawing lengths and angles of lines simultaneously. And make the largest cube that will fit on the page. If you can make these three ideas work together, the drawing will work (see Fig. 2-1).

At this point, you may be helped by knowing the principle of converging parallels. This idea comes from the study of perspective, the science of seeing. The

Figure 2-4. Parallel lines moving away from you appear to converge at a point on the eye level.

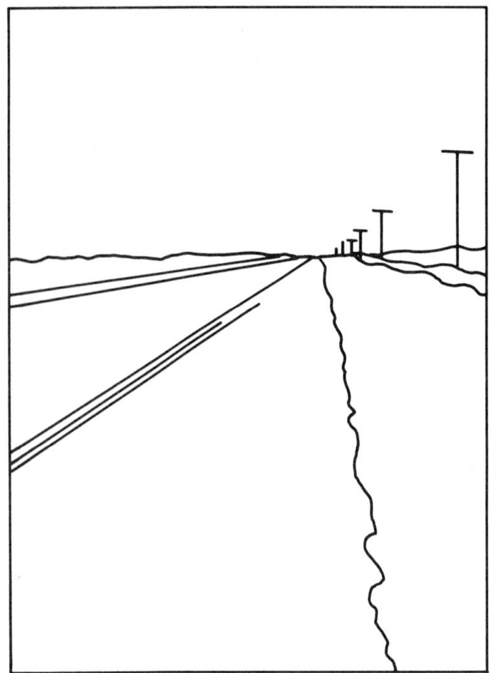

principle states that parallel lines moving away from you appear to converge at a point on the eye-level line (see Fig. 2-4). The cube you are drawing will have two systems of parallels that you'll need to deal with (three, including the vertical lines, but you don't need to worry about those as they will remain virtually parallel).

While the principle of converging parallels may help you understand what you are seeing, it should not be considered a substitute for looking at what is in front of you. *There is no substitute for observation.*

When measuring sizes and angles, ask yourself questions which force you to think of relationships: Is this line longer or shorter than that line? Is this angle more or less than 90 degrees? Which of these two angles is the most acute? Of all the angles, which is the most obtuse? Keep checking angle against angle and size against size until you are fairly satisfied that you have drawn the measurements as well as you can. An average time to spend on a line study of a cube might be one hour, but remember that it could take considerably more or less time depending on your experience and natural speed. Remember that you are measuring, not making pretty lines, and that the drawing is finished when the relationships are right.

When you have taken your drawing of the cube as far as you can, do a similar line study of a pyramid. Use the same approach as you used in your study of the cube. If you see that a line or an angle is no longer correctly proportioned for your drawing, take the time to make the necessary changes. A Pink Pearl eraser (or the equivalent) is the best eraser for pencil lines. Use it sparingly, but use it

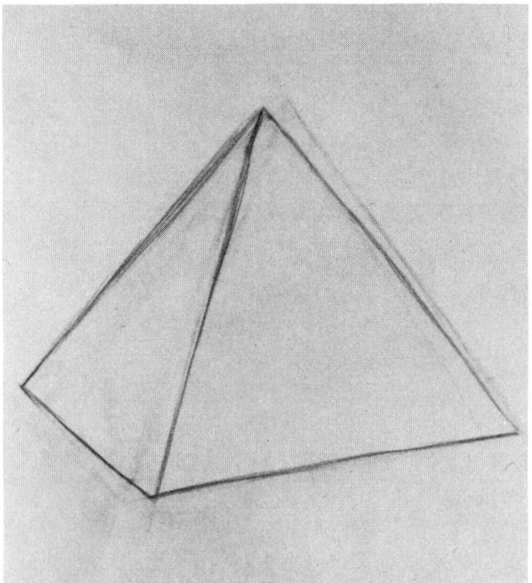

Figure 2-5. When measurements are off, take time to make necessary changes. Line drawing of a pyramid, by Ed Vick (computer science major). (Jean Mitchel).

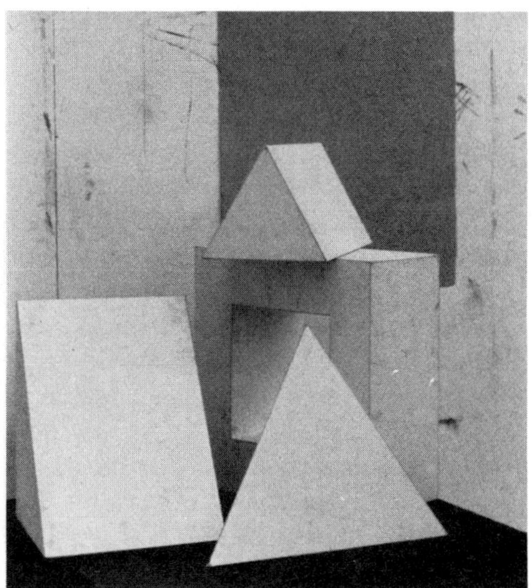

Figure 2-6. Overlapping planes, like converging parallels, help you to represent the illusion of three dimensional space on a two dimensional plane. (Lynn Martin)

when necessary. Sometimes errors in measurement will creep into your drawing no matter how much you have tried to keep them out, and their presence gives them an undeserved authority. So keep your lines light and searching. Light lines have a less committed feeling, as well as being physically easier to change. Remember: do no more than measure and place. Don't shade or put in accidental surface details. Working with a pure, simple, artless line will help you concentrate on getting relationships right and keeping the pyramid large on the page.

When you think you have completed the pyramid study, make a setup using several simple solids (Fig. 2-6) placed so that they partially conceal each other. Overlapping planes, like converging parallels, help you represent the illusion of three-dimensional space on a two-dimensional plane. Use the same approach for your drawing of this setup as

you used for the previous two drawings. You should be able to draw three or four objects in one-and-one-half to two hours.

VALUE

Value is the visualist's word for light and dark. Therefore, a value study is the study of the pattern of lights and darks seen in an object or group of objects. For your first value study, make an arrangement of a few simple solids with flat planes, such as a cube, a wedge, a pyramid. Leave the curved planes out of this set up. Arrange the forms so that they overlap each other as they did for your third line study. Shine a light onto one side of your arrangement or make sure it's near a window, so that one source of side light dominates all other sources of light. You should see only three or four major values: a lightest light, a darkest

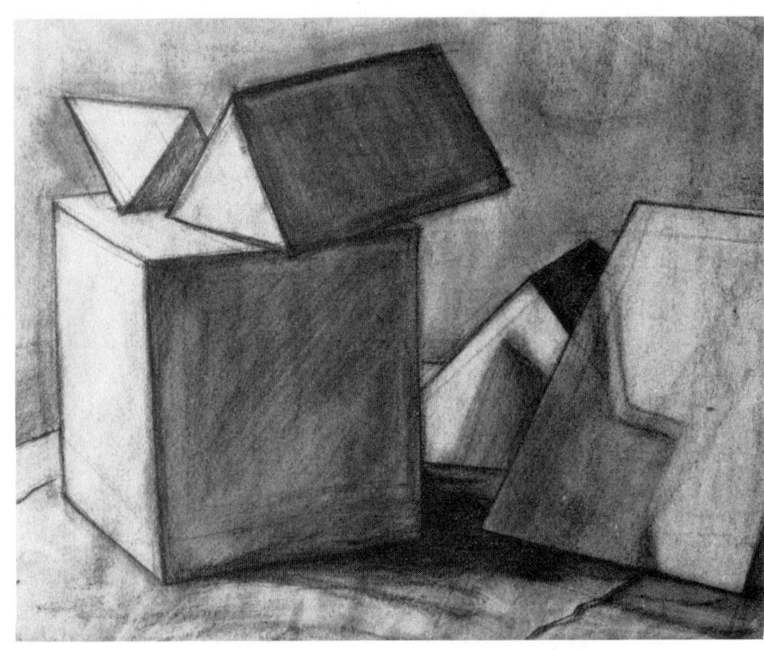

Figure 2-7. Construct your drawing with simple flat areas of values. Value study of flat planes, by Margaret Brinson (art education major). (Jean Mitchel).

dark, and one or two middle values. If you see more values than four, you will need to simplify your drawing by representing two darks, or lights, with the same value. Avoid looking for any nuances at this point. Construct your drawing with simple, flat planes.

Just as you have done with your previous studies, clamp a sheet of newsprint onto a drawing board on an easel adjusted to your standing height. You may need to use a two- or three-sheet thickness of newsprint so your drawing won't pick up any accidental texture from the surface of the drawing board. For each of the value studies you will need soft conté crayons, a chamois cloth, and a kneaded eraser. Start your drawing by putting a middle-value wash over the page by applying a fairly even tone with the side of a stick of conté (a half stick may be easier to work with), and then rub it around with a chamois cloth until

you have a consistent middle value covering the entire surface of your paper. Don't spend too much time on this stage of the drawing. Perfect smoothness is not necessary. Making the page a middle value is a purposeful part of the process, as it will help you see values. It will also cause you to *touch* every square inch of the surface of the page. This touch experience, along with the added practice of manipulating the conté and the chamois, leads painlessly into involvement with materials.

After applying the overall tone, do a somewhat hasty line drawing over the tone of the objects. Work as if you were making a very light version of your previous line drawings. Concentrate on size and angle measurement, and on placement. Your line drawing can be done with the end of your conté crayon or with a pencil. Once the line drawing is roughly established, start putting in the darkest planes and shadows with the side of the conté and taking out the light planes with a kneaded eraser. Pull and knead the eraser before you start; this will make it a more sensitive tool. Don't feel that you must follow the lines of your original drawing. Instead, check and recheck the proportions throughout the drawing process. Simultaneously, you are establishing the value pattern and trying to assess each plane of light and dark as well as you can. Keep working until you are satisfied that you have found the correct value relationships, the correct measurement of angle and size, and a comfortable relationship between the size of the objects and the size of the page. This study should take about two hours, although I have seen a few people work much longer on similar drawings. You shouldn't worry if it takes you longer, but at the same time you shouldn't make a lifetime project of your first value drawing.

You should have enough experience by this time to try a value study of a still life containing curved planes. Set up a group of solids as before, but this time include a cylinder, a cone, and a sphere as well. Curved planes present more subtle modulations of light than the flat planes you have been drawing. For instance, the darkest dark in the shadow of a cylinder is likely to be at the core of the shadow. In contrast, it would appear at the shadow's edge on a flat plane (see Fig. 2-8). In your drawings of flat planes you were asked to simplify the nuances of light or of dark into a few simple areas of value, so that your drawing would keep a clarity and a sense of purpose as a diagram of the phenomenon of light playing on objects. This is as important, if not more so, in your study of curved planes. You are apt to notice the most subtle gradations of value caused by reflections picked up by the curves. It will be your job to find the lights and darks which describe volume in space and to leave out all those changes which are superficial.

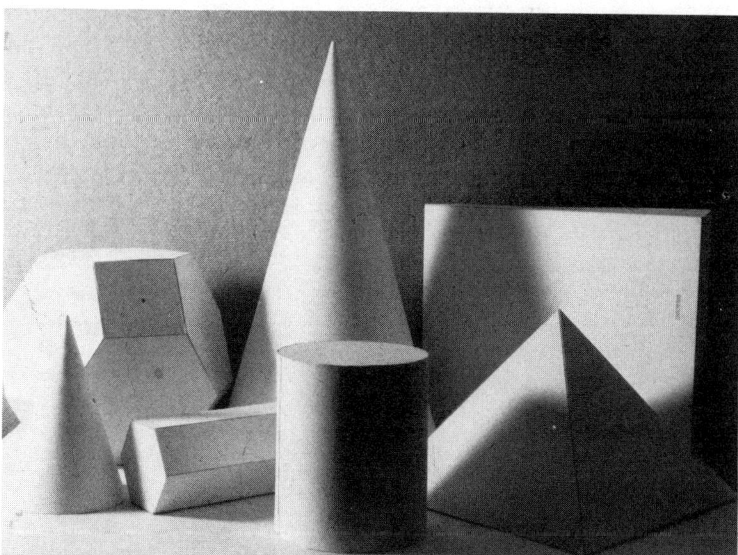

Figure 2-8. Curved planes present more subtle modulations of light than flat planes. (Jean Mitchel).

The two student drawings, Figs. 2-9 and 2-10, are competent value studies of objects with curved planes. These drawings go further in manipulation of materials and in stylistic treatment than such studies need to go. The student who drew them could measure and compose competently; therefore, it was acceptable to me that she incorporated textural treatment and style into her works. You can give yourself the same freedom *if* you are sure that your ability to measure and place are far enough along. But never try to get ahead of yourself. Never manipulate materials or indulge in technical tricks you may have seen someone else do to cover up a lazy attitude toward measuring. By doing so, you could be denying yourself the solid foundation that is so necessary for your future growth.

The elliptical planes that occur at the ends of cylinders present a common problem in drawing. In Fig. 2-11, the ellipse diagrammed as a circle charted in perspective is a continuous curve. Some beginners have a tendency to bring the left and right sides of an ellipse to points. For the sake of your drawing, it is worth the time it takes to carefully study the nature of the curves in an ellipse. Look at the carefully worked, slightly irregular

opening of the horn in the Kuhn painting (Fig. 2-12). Realist painting is rich with such examples. And yet I have noticed that some of the applicants to the graduate school where I teach are still drawing flower pots and the like with tops that are pointed.

You may be able to work comfortably for two or more hours on this study of flat and curved planes, but the comments already made concerning individual time needs apply here and in subsequent studies.

Much can be learned, especially about volume in space, from the study of geometric solids. This understanding will serve you later on in far more complex drawings. It will help solidify the quick studies that you will work on in the next chapter. But a steady diet of white abstract forms may soon become boring to you—not enough challenge, not enough variety—and you will want to do a study of objects that are more familiar to you from everyday experience. Tools, kitchen utensils, simple lamps, baskets, musical instruments—any of these would carry through the idea of symmetrical solids, while offering a relief from the stark simplicity of geometry. Perhaps you can think of some other category of found

Figures 2-9 and **2-10.** Value studies of flat and curved planes, by Joan Blakemore (art education major). (Jean Mitchel).

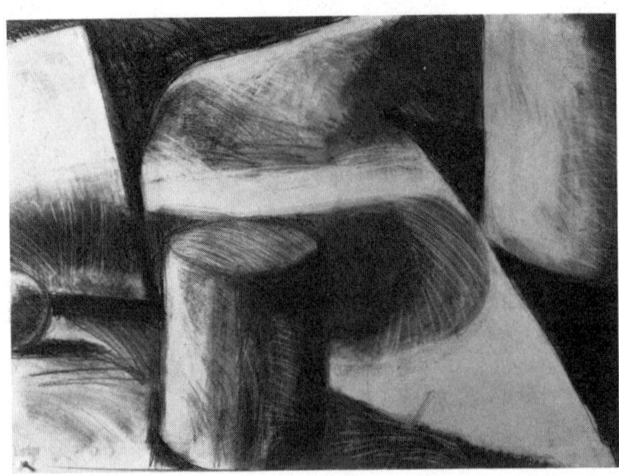

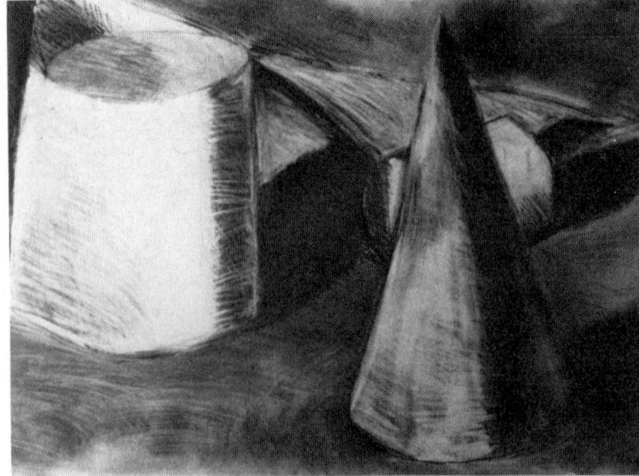

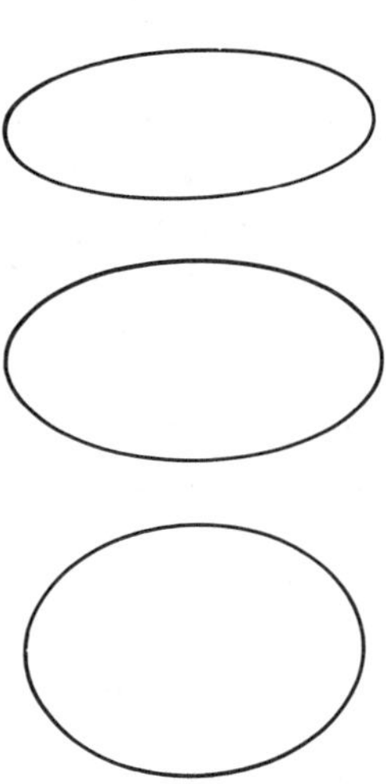

Figure 2-11. The line of the ellipse is a continuous curve.

Figure 2-12. The opening of the horn is a carefully worked, slightly irregular ellipse. *Musical Clown,* by Walt Kuhn. 1938. Oil on canvas, 40″ × 30″. (Whitney Museum of American Art, New York).

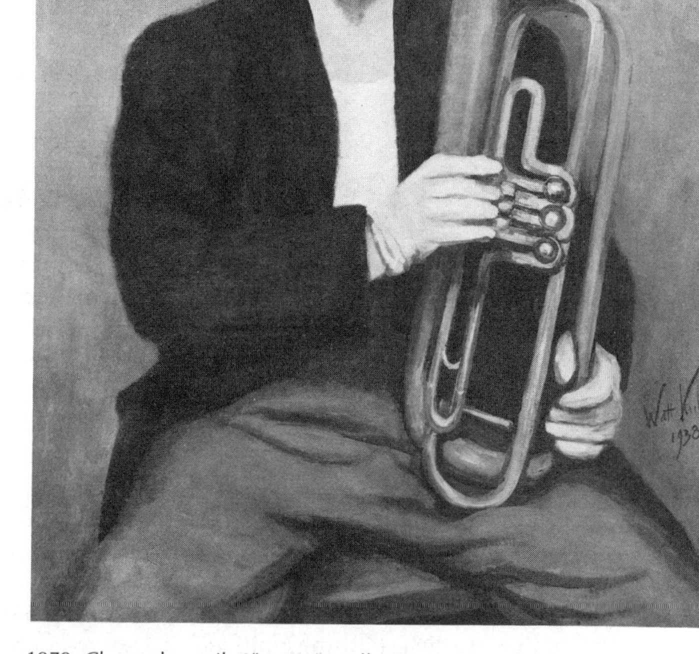

Figure 2-13. *Soap,* by Alfred Martinez. 1979. Charcoal pencil, 8″ × 10″. Collection of the artist. (Diana Ault).

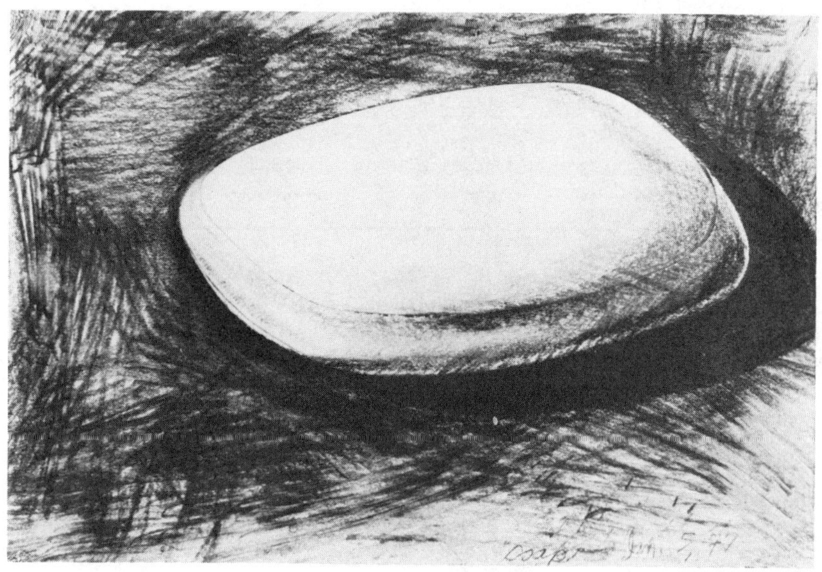

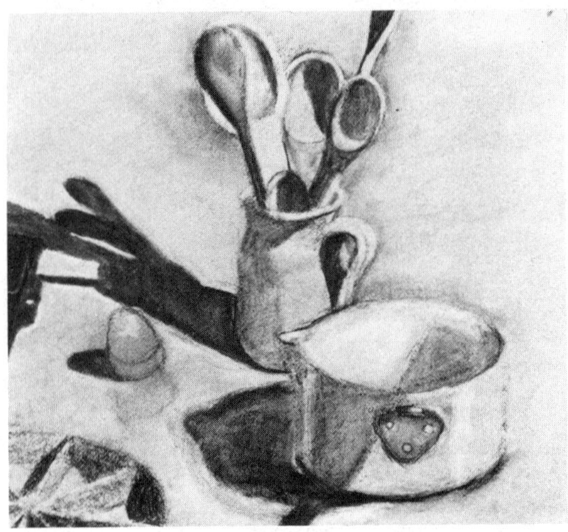

Figure 2-14. Kitchen utensils carry through the idea of symmetrical solids while offering a relief from the starkness of geometry. Value study of a still life, by Jonah Winter (English major). (author).

objects that will serve the purpose as well as the ones I mention (see Fig. 2-14).

A still-life arrangement with such objects should utilize the side lighting as described earlier. Make your drawing by using the same process as you did in the previous value studies, limiting yourself to a minimum of values and to two or three hours work.

This is the first time you will need to draw objects whose value difference may be caused as much by pigmentation as by light. Although you may not be able to avoid seeing the values occurring from the different colors, you should make an effort to see what light is doing to the forms. It is through light that you are able to see volume. Respond to the play of light on objects, and your drawing will be more solid.

While I suggest spending two to three hours on this study, you should remember that to some extent the complexity of your arrangement will determine the time you need.

Organic forms such as vegetables and fruits make a natural progression from the forms with symmetrical, "perfect" planes you have been drawing toward the asymmetrical character of the posed model. Also, as familiar as an apple, a pear, or an eggplant may be to you, you may discover after a session of drawing them that you never really looked at these objects before. Their basic struc-

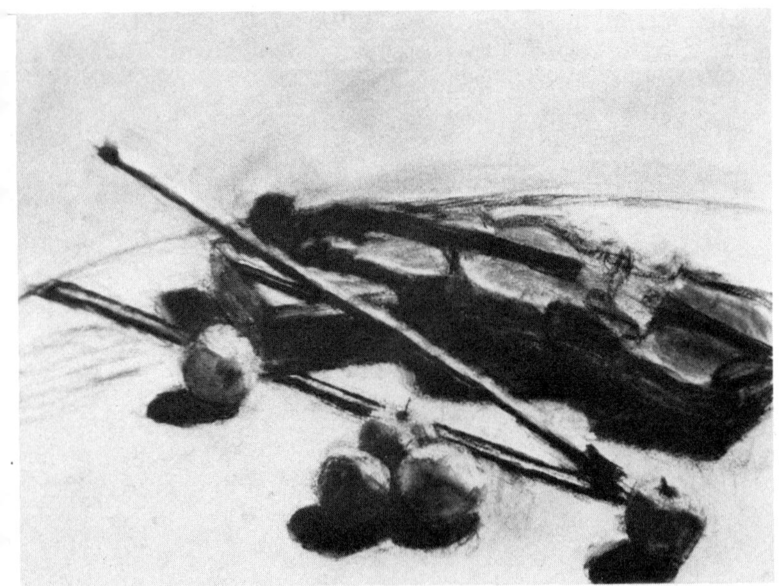

Figure 2-15. Value study of a still life, by Jonah Winter (English major). (author).

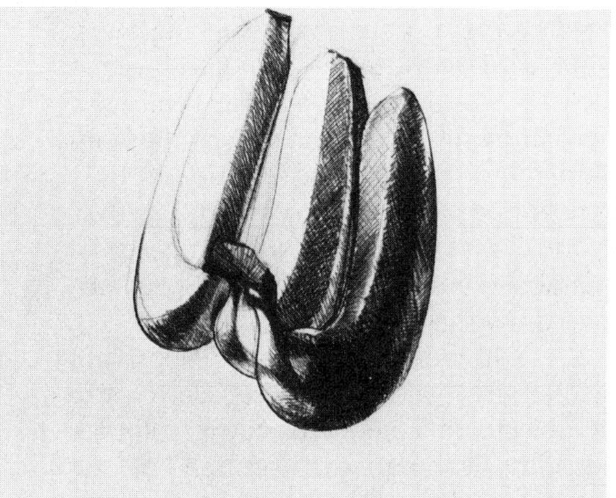

Figure 2-16. *Bananas,* by Alfred Martinez. 1979. Charcoal pencil, 22″ × 28″. Collection of the artist. (Diana Ault).

tures and the subtleties of their surface planes may be a welcome relief from the machine-made objects of previous setups.

For a first drawing of fruits and vegetables, keep your arrangement simple—perhaps no more than three or four items. You may wish to make a more complex second arrangement, emphasizing texture, contrasting shapes, lines, and so forth. Again, use the same procedural approach for these studies as you have in the other value drawings.

For a class project in measuring values, cut up a black-and-white reproduction of a well-known painting into as many squares as there are students in a class or group. Assign one square to each student, and give each student the same instructions: Make an accurate value study of the square at a given dimension. Each study should be the same size, done with the same tool (a No. 2B drawing pencil, for instance), on the same type of paper. Emphasize that the values in the study must be the same as the values in the assigned square. No one needs to know what the squares represent, since knowing might damage objectivity. When all

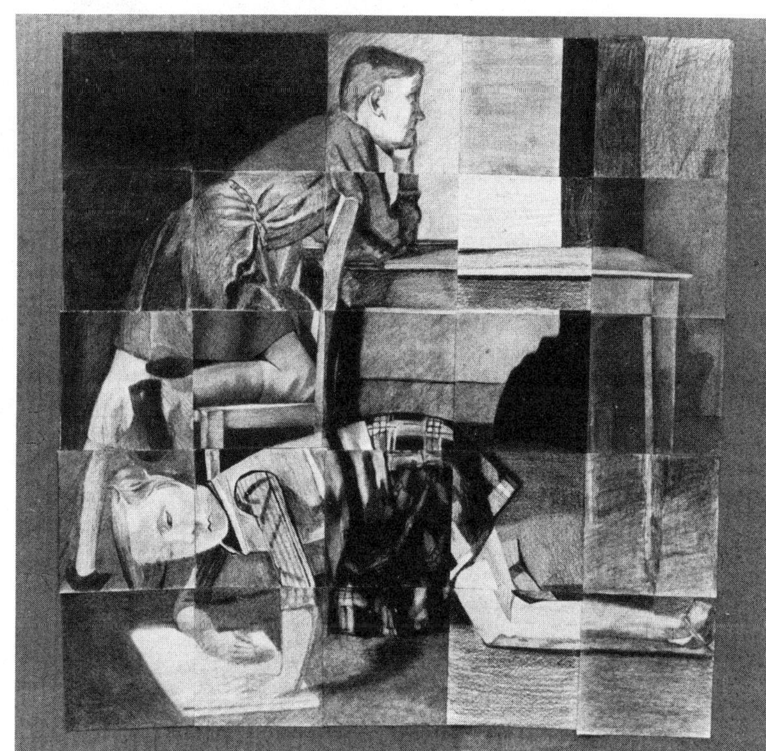

Figure 2-17. Class project in measuring values. Pencil study of *The Children,* by Balthus. Each square 4″ × 4″. (Lynn Martin).

the squares are returned, reconstruct the original painting by pinning up the squares in their relative places. Any square whose values are off will look obviously out of place in the reconstruction. These "off" squares should be drawn again until the transition across the reconstruction is smooth.

SUMMARY

Before you start to draw, you should be aware that seeing *and* placing are of equal importance to drawing. Also, try to form helpful habits right at the beginning, such as standing at your easel, backing away from your work to get a more objective look at it, and facing your paper and the objects being studied. You should keep your mind on the exercise, but don't expect your drawing to look exactly like everyone else's drawing. Your own personal characteristics will show even in your earliest drawings.

You not only measure sizes, but also angles, values, and the relative size of objects to page. Measuring calls for constant comparison through asking questions about relationships. The progression in drawing method is from line to value, and from setups of geometric solids to organic form.

Chapter 3
QUICK STUDIES

There is always a bigger truth undiscovered—unsaid—uncharted until you meet it.

Kimon Nicolaides

FROM SUSTAINED WORK TO QUICK STUDIES

In Chapter 2 you learned to make a deliberate drawing along specific guidelines with a comfortable amount of time to complete each work. This is an important approach to learning to see and to draw. But it is only one of two basic approaches. The second approach is to do quick studies. As sustained studies exercise the eye, the conscious mind, and the critical sense, quick studies bring intuition and feeling into use. Experienced drawing teachers know that the two methods combined build on each other. The sustained work brings knowledge and grasp to the quick studies; the quick studies give life and freedom to the sustained work. Quick and sustained, the two basic methods in drawing, will constitute a working pattern throughout this book.

INTUITION

The discovery of one's intuitive power is one of the significant, often unexpected benefits gained by drawing. It is always preceded by a complete turning loose of the normal fears that cause the overcontrol and hesitancy in a beginner's work.

Spontaneity, or the willingness to *be* spontaneous, does not come easily to everyone. And why should it? From infancy, we are taught to "behave" ourselves, to resist showing our true feelings. In school, neatness counts and scribbling is bad. We are taught to control the way we look, talk, walk, and eat. It is no wonder that many of us reach adult age with a highly developed surface control and a serious concern over what might happen should the surface control ever be abandoned.

To get an idea of what it's like to "let go" and do quick studies, it may be helpful to look at the quick work of great artists like Rembrandt (Figs. 3-1 and 3-2). The fluid, spontaneous, free, and expressive nature of his drawings comes as a surprise to many students who only know his paintings. These studies are the mother and father of his sustained work in painting, although the relationship may not be apparent at first. Parallel situations can be found in the drawings of Delacroix, Poussin, Goya, da Vinci, Degas, Daumier, de Kooning, and Diebenkorn— to name a few. Their quick drawings

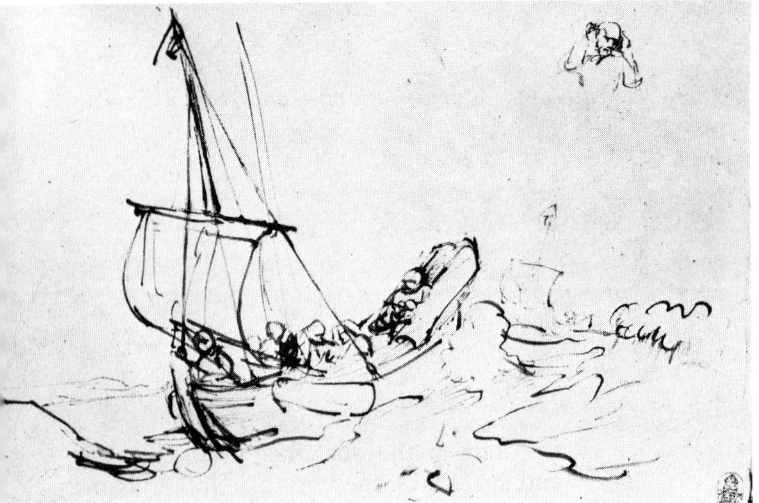

Figure 3-1. *Christ in the Storm on the Sea of Galilee,* by Rembrandt Van Rijn. c. 1654–55. Pen and bistre, 7¾" × 11⅘". (Kupferstich-Kabinett, Dresden).

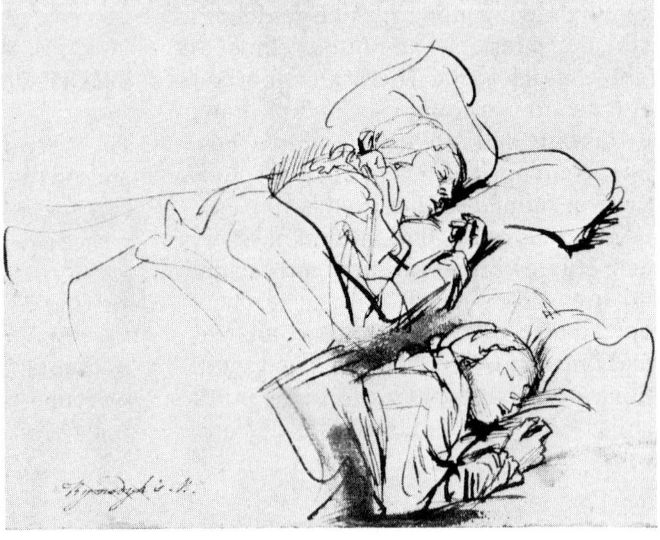

Figure 3-2. *Two Studies of Saskia Asleep in Bed,* by Rembrandt Van Rijn. c. 1635. Pen, brush, and bistre, 5⅛" × 6¾". (Pierpont-Morgan Library, New York).

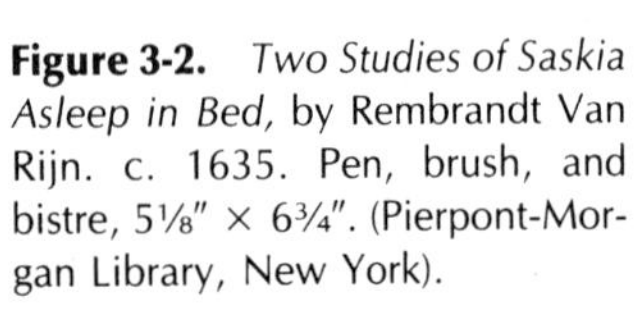

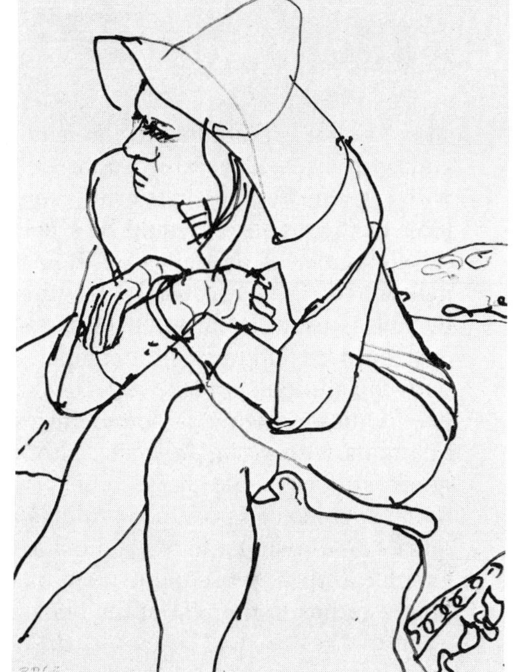

Figure 3-3. Pen-and-ink drawing, by Richard Diebenkorn. 1963. 17" × 12½". Collection of the artist. (Richard Diebenkorn).

Figure 3-4. *The Massacre of the Innocents,* by Nicolas Poussin. Pen and brown ink with some wash, 5¾" × 6⅔". Reprinted, with permission, from Anthony Blunt, *The Drawings of Poussin* (Yale University Press, New Haven).

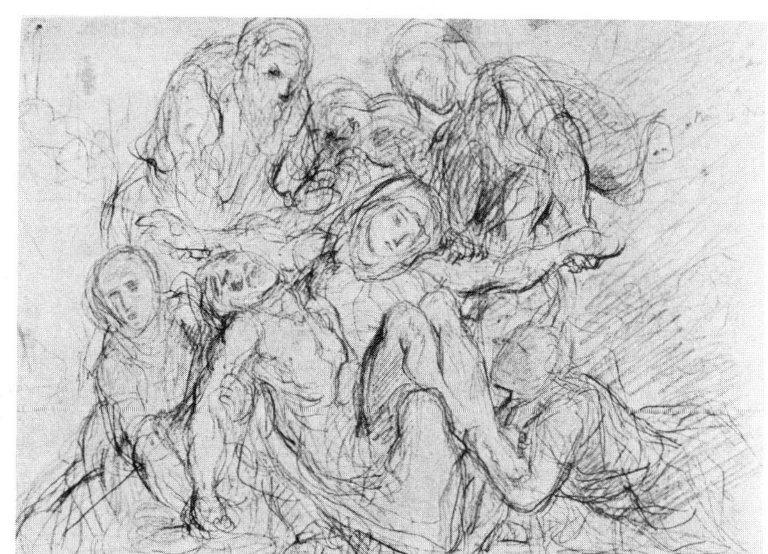

Figure 3-5. *Study for the ''Pieta'',* by Eugene Delacroix. 1830. Pencil. (The Louvre, Paris).

show us the explorations of their minds and spirits, as ideas are caught on the wing by the free but masterful drawing tools of the artists. It would be a helpful class excercise if drawings by the artists mentioned (the list could be lengthened by miles) could be brought to class—in any reproduction form—for comparisons with the students' quick works.

Quick drawing is sometimes synonymous with *gesture drawing*, although quick studies could have other intentions, such as compositional studies and quick line drawings. In the context of this chapter and in subsequent mentions of quick studies in the rest of the book, the quality of gesture will be *a part* of drawing quickly.

The concept of gesture goes far back into Western art and academic training. Parallel concepts are essential to oriental painting and drawing. But the modern student exercise called gesture drawing is inevitably based on the idea of gesture as presented by Kimon Nicolaides in his famous book *The Natural Way to Draw*. Nicolaides viewed gesture drawing as far more than the loosening up exercise it often becomes in life drawing classes. He saw it as the very essence of drawing; as a most worthwhile search in the drawing room:

> *Quick sketches are often used simply to "loosen up" the student and not as a means of penetrating study. Often students do them well and are quite surprised at the results, which are far beyond any knowledge they have. The reason is that by working quickly they accidentally find the gesture. The gesture is a feeler which reaches out and guides them to knowledge.*
>
> *Kimon Nicolaides*

The search in gesture drawing is to find the *verbs* of a figure or object while using a minimum of nouns and adjectives. In other words, look for the model's stride, slump, and grasp, and forget about the elbow, the skin, the color, and the hair style.

Before you try quick studies, see if you can manage to watch some experienced students go through a session of gesture drawings from a model. It would be helpful if the same group of students could then watch *you* draw right at the beginning, setting you on the right course before harmful habits are formed.

As Nicolaides pointed out, you may find that you can do these drawings surprisingly well, and you may receive praise from your teacher or from the other students. But no matter how proud you feel about your early efforts, I caution you not to show your first gesture drawings to well-meaning family members or friends. The early stages of learning to draw are delicate, and you could have your confidence, even your desire, destroyed by harsh remarks from someone who doesn't understand what you are trying to accomplish. It would be better to wait until your

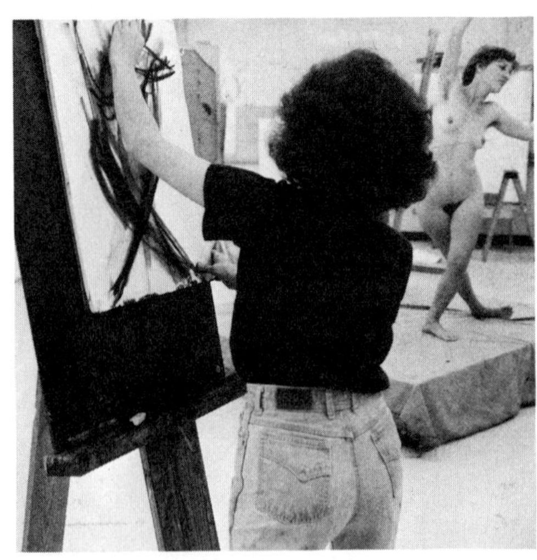

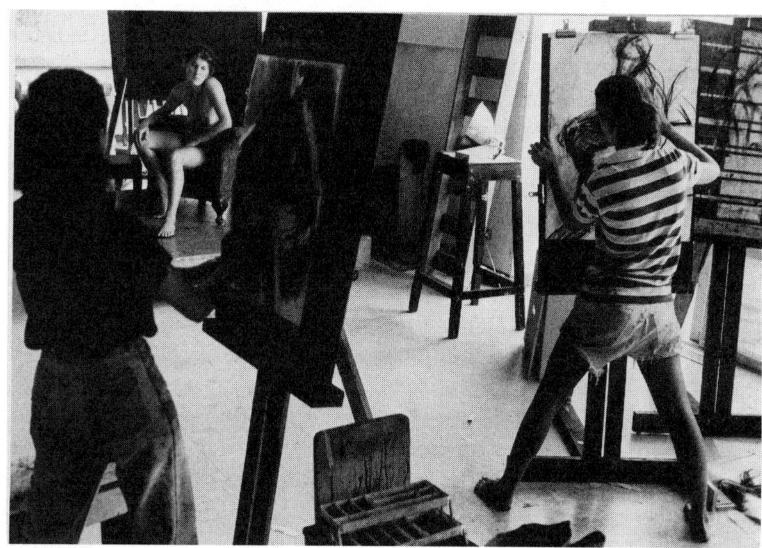

Figure 3-7. If possible, watch some experienced students draw. (author).

work is in a class exhibit (or other group exhibit) before inviting outside friends to see it. Here, in the proper context, your work is more likely to be a learning experience for the viewer, and you will be able to maintain a better perspective on what you have learned and are moving toward in your drawing.

THE MODEL

A nude model is the best possible model for quick studies, not only because we empathize so readily with human form but also because of the intelligence and flexibility of the model. A model can run through thirty interesting one-minute poses without pause, while a chair, a shoe, or any other object is a static form not able to respond to the artist's needs. All objects have gesture (see Fig. 3-8), and you should study their gestures for the sake of variety, if for no other reason. But during the early stages of learning to draw, no object should supplant a live

model stripped of the cuffs, collars, buttons, and other details of clothing a beginner is likely to see instead of the more important structure.

A good model knows that he or she is working for the class, and therefore strives to take interesting poses and hold them steadily for the specified length of

Figure 3-8. All objects have gesture. *Study #1*, by James Dowell. 1981. Black and white conte crayon, 9½″ × 10″. Collection of the artist. (James Dowell).

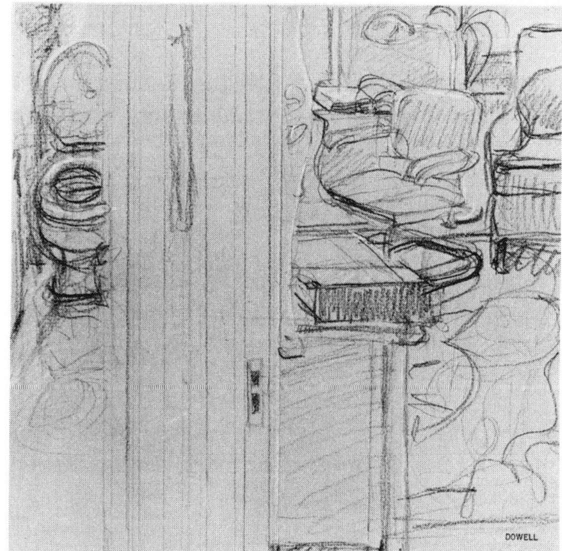

time. A good model can be quite an asset to a drawing class; on the other hand, a model who talks to the class while posing, yawns and moves around, doesn't understand what is needed, or brings ego problems to the model stand is both frustrating and time-wasting for those drawing. A class has every right to expect professionalism from its models. Modeling is far more than taking one's clothes off. I often ask each member of my class to take a few poses for quick studies so that the idea of gesture *and* the role of the model can be better understood.

The best poses for quick studies are poses with strong diagonal movement. In standing poses the feet of the model should be striding or otherwise interestingly placed, avoiding the symmetrical. The spine should be angled, twisted, or both; the neck and head, tilted; the face turned to one side. The head should never be held straight over the shoulders. Such a position creates a static force that inhibits the rhythmic movement so needed in the process of quick drawing.

The model should be able to go through thirty quick poses without any pauses in between. The question, "What should I do now?" coming from a model in the middle of a session of quick poses is frustrating to the class and to the teacher. If the model needs suggestions for new poses, he or she should bring the subject up during a break or before or after class. It could be useful to the model and the class to ask the model to imitate poses found in paintings, drawings, or sculpture. Complimenting models after a session of good poses is one way to reassure them that their performance is appreciated and inspiring.

Remind the model to rotate the poses so that no one person gets all frontal poses, another all back poses, and so on. Also, the poses should vary as much as possible from seated to standing to reclining. While in one pose the model can decide the direction of the next pose.

THE PROCESS

Quick drawings should be done at the beginning of a three-hour session with a model. A typical time pattern might be to do 25 to 30 one-minute drawings followed by a sustained study based on whatever ideas the class may be dealing with at a given time.

In this chapter I give the procedures for quick studies done with pencil, conté, brush and ink, and clay. In subsequent chapters, as quick drawing exercises related to the ideas under study, I will introduce scissors and paper, collage, chamois, and mixed media. The process will not always be the same, but the need for spontaneity and an overall treatment will be encouraged regardless of material.

Pencil

Your first quick studies will be done in No. 6B (or other soft leaded) pencil on 12″ × 18″ newsprint. Ask the model to take a series of 25 to 30 one-minute poses. Clamp thirty sheets of newsprint to a masonite panel placed on an easel. Plan on using both sides of your paper before discarding any drawings—to do otherwise is not only a waste of money but of the wood the paper was made from. When the model assumes the first pose, start to move your pencil around and around the page, following the lines of movement in the model. Make long, circular motions. Don't scratch. Leave the

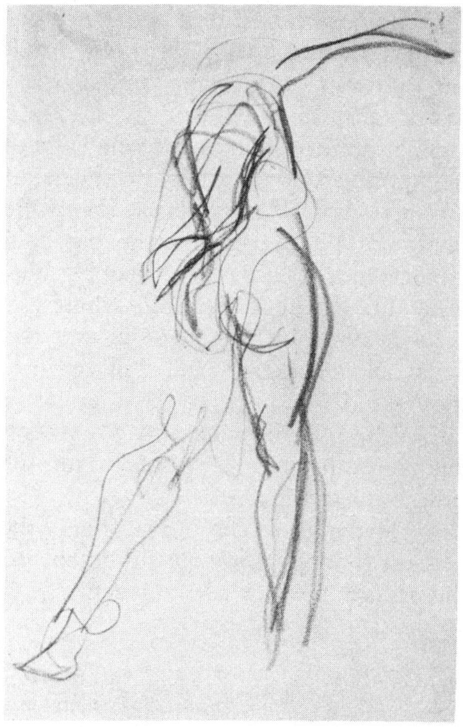

Figure 3-9. Make long, circular motions. Don't scratch. Quick study, by Joan Blakemore (art education major). (Jean Mitchel)

pencil on the paper and let it roam freely over the page, moving from top to bottom, from side to side, from head to foot, and back again for the full time of the pose. Draw lines across and around the middle of the form. Avoid outlines. Gesture has no outlines just as the force of the wind has no outlines. *Let the drawing breathe*; don't imprison it with hard boundaries. Be excessive; exaggerate; distort. Put energy into the work. Work on the whole form. Above all, don't start the drawing at the top of the head and work down. Start it with that aspect of the overall form which you feel is the most critical revelation of the essence of the pose. If the model is reaching over and touching the floor, draw the whole movement of the body from the toes and feet up and around and down again to the fingertips. Get this much drawn before you try to elaborate on any lesser aspect of the gesture, such as the gesture of the hair or the fingers. Any other approach will start you off on the wrong track and will only waste your practice time.

As you gain confidence with quick studies you can ask the model to take poses of various lengths, from five seconds to one minute. At the start, however, limit the poses to one minute each so that a dependable rhythm is maintained.

Conté

After one or two sessions of quick drawing with pencil, switch to conté crayon. Conté will be bolder, freer, and more

Figure 3-10. Quick study, by Susan Johnson (art major). (author).

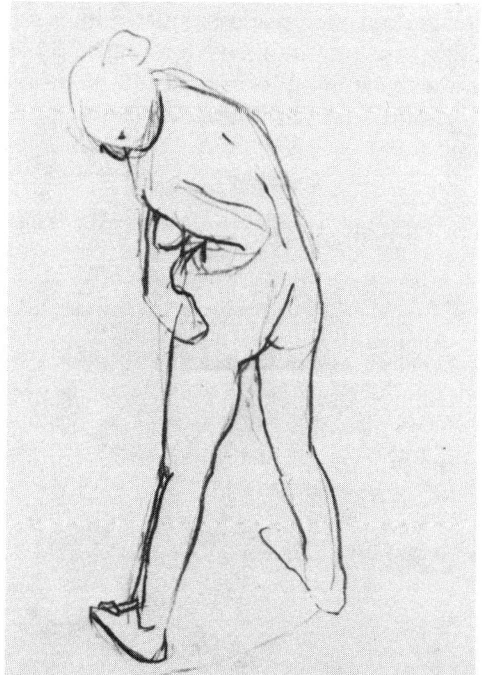

atmospheric than pencil. Don't try to make conté a rough substitute for pencil. Learn to let it be itself. Use the side of the crayon as well as its ends. Try to get the feeling of the material—see what makes it special. Go to a library or to a museum and look up the conté drawings by Seurat. Emulate the soft edges (see Fig. 5-12) and feeling of light while you are doing your quick studies. Or look at the drawings of Maillol or Renoir. In order to get the feeling of conté or of any other material you not only have to use it but you also have to find out how others have used it.

Just as you did in the quick studies with pencil, think about the movement, or the *verbs*, in the pose. Remember that the model is occupying three-dimensional space, so try to draw the movement in space. Once again, your eyes should be moving around and around, from side to side, and from top to bottom—even outside the model into the surrounding space. You should be getting the idea by this time that quick studies are not just exercises in freedom, despite the spontaneous approach. They are a disciplined form of study requiring constant alertness, total concentration, and great courage.

Brush and Ink

Every material has its essence. Pencil is dry and linear. Conté is airy. The essence of ink is its flowing quality, and a bamboo brush uses ink's wetness and flow to the fullest. A bamboo brush (medium or large) keeps a sensitive record of your hesitancy or boldness. Don't try to change the nature of this medium. Let it have its way. Be positive. The results of

a bold approach with ink and brush are wonderful to see (Fig. 5-15), while drawings done with a hesitant approach can be a painful sight. Never try to use a brush and ink as if you were using a pencil. Nothing but nagging little mistakes can come from this approach. Hold the brush out by the end; make big bold strokes; and, if necessary, make big mistakes until you get to the point where you really understand the material and feel comfortable using it. You will come to understand that drips and spatters are a natural part of the medium—an acceptable byproduct of your search for the movement of the model.

Have a jar or can of water near the ink so that you can keep the brush wet and dilute the ink as you sense it is needed.

Figure 3-11. Make big, bold strokes. Brush-and-ink study, by Marilu Gruben (art education major). (Jean Mitchel).

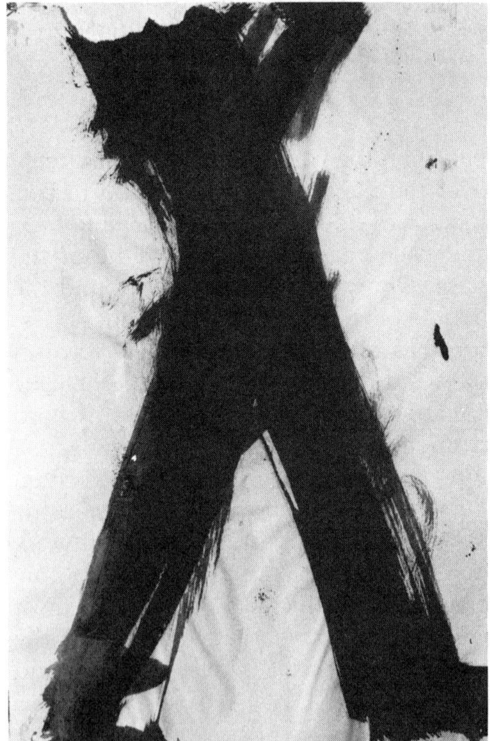

Clay

The fastest way to learn to see gesture in space is to make some quick clay studies of a model. The nature of drawing with clay forces you to move around and around the model, seeing the model from virtually hundreds of points of view. I have found two exercises with clay that adapt easily to a drawing room. Both are relatively quick—one takes no more than five minutes; the other, thirty minutes.

For the five-minute studies you will need a 15- to 20-pound bag of modeling clay and a strand of wire with short pieces of dowels attached to each end as handles. With the wire, cut off several pieces of clay, each about the size of a baseball. Ask the model to take a series of 6 or 7 five-minute poses. They must be seated or reclining poses, since standing poses require a means of support for the clay. With a piece of clay in your hands, start to move around and around the model; shaping the hand-held clay from every possible angle, looking for the gesture of the model. It is essential that you stay on the move. To stand in one place too long would simply defeat the purpose of the exercise. Be alert; moving almost constantly, working the clay with your hands, and making quick adjustments from every new view of the model. Keep your mind on the total pose. Don't worry about how the study will look, since most of these studies (if not all) will be torn down to make works of the next session of poses. You may want to keep a few of them around for a day or two so that you can learn from their virtues and flaws. Just remember that these are only studies, not art objects, and that you don't need to feel precious about them.

The thirty-minute approach is still a quick study, considering the medium. The process is somewhat the same as in the five-minute studies, except that you will need a clay-modeling stand for the thirty-minute studies so you can stabilize your slightly larger, somewhat more involved work as you move around the model. Also, you may want to use a sling tool (a small wooden stick with a wire loop at one or both ends) or even a stick or other homemade tool to flatten planes and cut recesses into the study. Keep your mind on gesture, pose, and movement. It would be needless to try to explore the surface details of the form before you fully understand the *glue* the

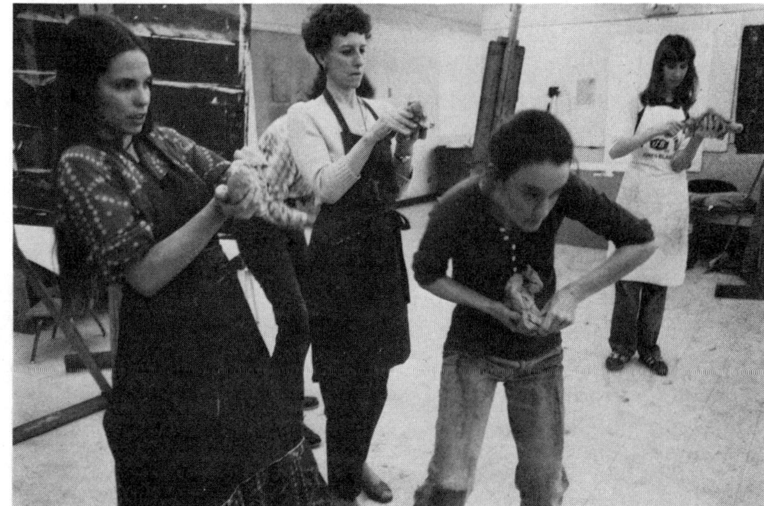

Figure 3-12. Stay on the move, making adjustments in your clay study from every new view of the model. (Lynn Martin).

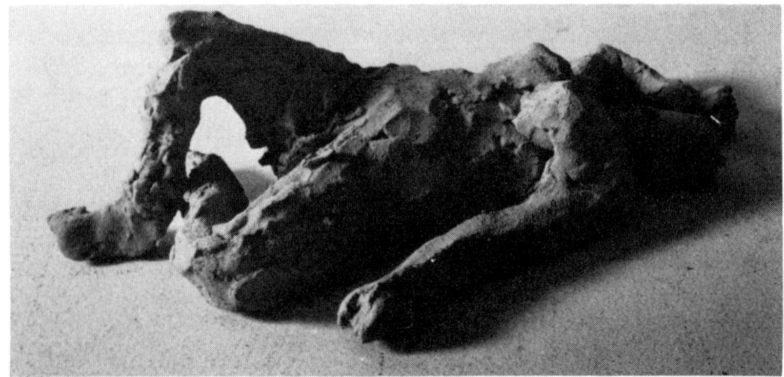

Figure 3-13. Let the surface of the clay stay rough and alive. Thirty-minute clay study, by Julie Hausman (art major). (Jean Mitchel).

spirit—which unifies the form. Work in the most general way. Avoid specifics. Let the surface of the clay stay rough and alive. If you have a tendency to smooth it out, resist—emphasizing the skin might cause you to lose sight of gesture and structure.

Keep in mind that unless you have access to a kiln and you want to go to the trouble of hollowing out your pieces to a ½ inch shell so that they can be fired, these works will likely be torn up for subsequent studies or discarded. So don't think of them as permanent. They are just studies, and like a musician's practice sessions, they are aimed at increasing your ability. Clay is a fine material for more involved sculptural ideas, but you don't have to use it that way; nor must you think of what you do as sculpture. Just draw with it, and let others use it in their way.

VARIATIONS ON QUICK STUDIES

If you should find that you are having trouble loosening up enough to do the fast poses, or if you just want some variety in approaching quick studies, ask the model to take a series of moving poses. The model should move back and forth through two or three positions, as if exercising, holding each stage for a second or two before moving on to the next stage. Each separate series of moving poses should be done over and over for two to three minutes. While drawing a moving pose, *look at the model*. Make sure

Figure 3-14. Study of moving pose, by Marilu Gruben (art education major). (Jean Mitchel).

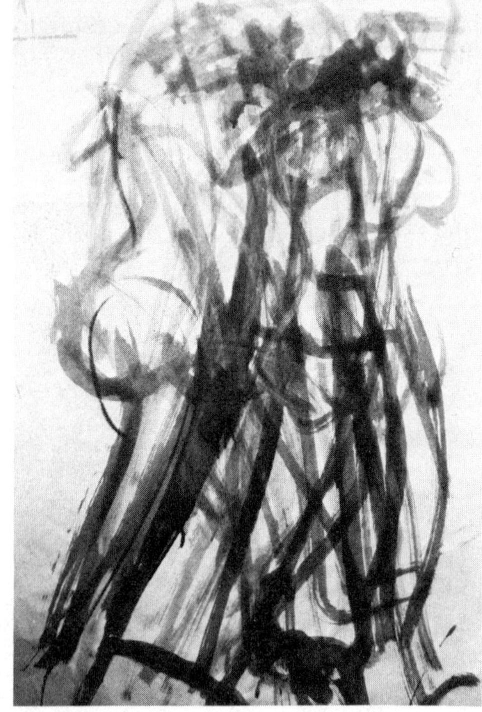

your material keeps up with the model. Let your pencil (or other material) roam across the page, following the movements of the model. Above all, don't try to "make a drawing." Just follow the model with your eyes and your hand and arm. Let go. You can't do this exercise if you are too tight.

Another good variation on poses for quick drawings is the group pose. The most important thing to remember when drawing a group of figures (perhaps two to four members of a class posing together) is to draw them all at once, using an overall approach. Always look for the unifying rhythm of movements and

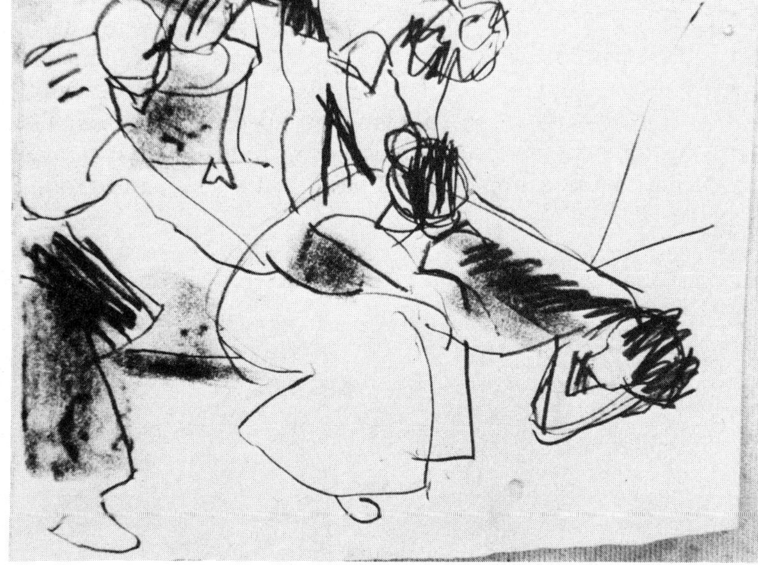

Figure 3-15. Look for the unifying rhythms of movements and shapes. Quick study of group pose, by Mary Elizabeth Howard (art major). (author).

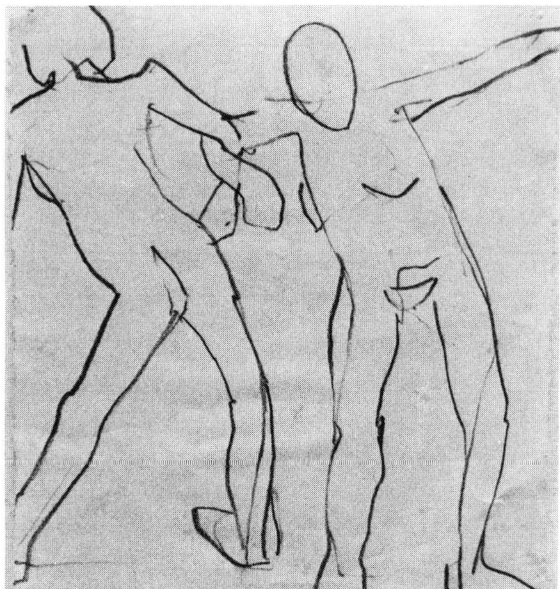

Figure 3-16. Group poses will help you see relationships. Quick study of group pose, by Susan Johnson (art major). (author).

shapes. In other words, look only for those forces which are tying the group together. *Don't draw one figure at a time.* Nothing could be more harmful to your drawing at this stage, since it would condition you to draw in a piecemeal fashion. If you look for the overall, for unity, you may find that group poses help you more than a single figure in seeing relationships.

SUMMARY

The capacity to be spontaneous, to use intuitive power, can be blocked by thinking that you must always be in control. Often newcomers to quick drawing feel the authority to turn loose and take chances after watching experienced students at work and looking at the spontaneous drawings of the masters, old and new.

Procedural approaches to quick drawing differ somewhat, depending upon whether you are using dry material, ink, or clay. But regardless of the material being used, quick studies always call for a spontaneous, overall approach.

Once you have gained confidence with five-second to one-minute poses, you can vary the idea with moving poses and group poses.

Chapter 4
THE PAGE

TWO-DIMENSIONAL SPACE

Awareness of the page is of crucial importance in retaining, throughout a drawing, the purity and strength of the rectangular form with which one begins. The thrust of this chapter is to heighten that awareness through discussion of the components of the page and through exercises involving the study of composition.

Open Space

Just as a musician must work with silence as well as sound, so must the visual artist understand the usefulness of open space in a drawing. The haunting studies by Bill Komodore and William Bailey (Figs. 4-1 and 4-2) are poignant examples of works by two artists who understand the expressive possibilities of

Figure 4-1. *Norma,* by Bill Komodore. 1976. Pencil, 22¾" × 30". Collection of Oz and Paul Srere, Dallas. (Jean Mitchel).

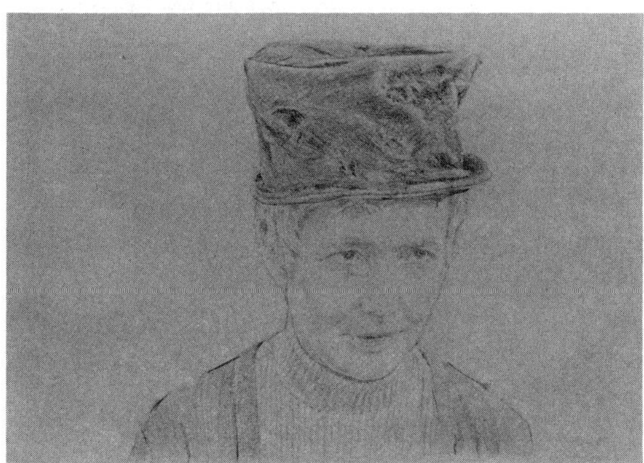

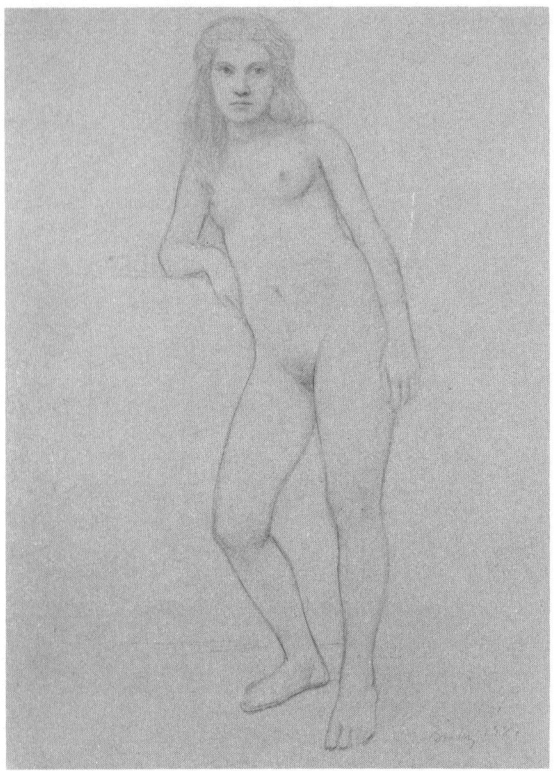

Figure 4-2. *Standing Figure,* by William Bailey. 1980. Pencil on paper, 14″ × 11″. (Robert Schoelkopf Gallery, Ltd., New York).

the emptiness and luminosity of white paper. In each work deep space is suggested by the use of a figure, but the two-dimensionality of the page is not lost. The drawings do not become holes. For both artists the white rectangular surface of paper seems to have an almost holy significance.

The Picture Plane

The deep space in traditional Western painting is alien to much of Eastern art. If we compare Mu Ch'i's *The Six Persimmons* with Thomas Cole's *Pic–Nic*, we begin to realize how concerned with spatial illusion Cole must have been (Figs. 4-3 and 4-4). Cole's painting is like a window, and it leads our eye back into space. In contrast, the Mu Ch'i painting *confronts* us with two-dimensional space. The forms in the painting relate to each other on the surface plane—the picture plane. Modern Western painters also place a priority on keeping the surface plane intact. Even in recent illusionistic works such as Fairfield Porter's *October Interior* (Fig. 4-5) you can sense a respect for the intrinsic value of the various visual elements—the relation of the positive shapes of objects to the negative background shapes, the variation of the scale of shapes in the pattern, and the simplicity of the planal construction—as they interact on the two-dimensional surface of the canvas. Porter's retention of the picture plane shows the lessons he learned from the structural principles of early modern art.

Early abstract artists* felt an intensely fervent drive to free European painters and sculptors from the tradition of illusionism they had known for so long. Simple geometric forms and their relationships on flat planes (Fig. 4-6) provided a natural source for many early modern painters who were breaking away from illusionism. Geometry has in so many times and places held the imagination of people, and has often symbol-

* Although the phrase *abstract art* is synonymous in popular usage with modern art, abstraction is a process that goes on at all times in illusionistic painting as the three-dimensionality of nature is transferred to the two-dimensional space of a canvas or page. *Non-objective* is a more accurate description of art that attempts to abide by its own laws and take nothing from the surface appearance of nature.

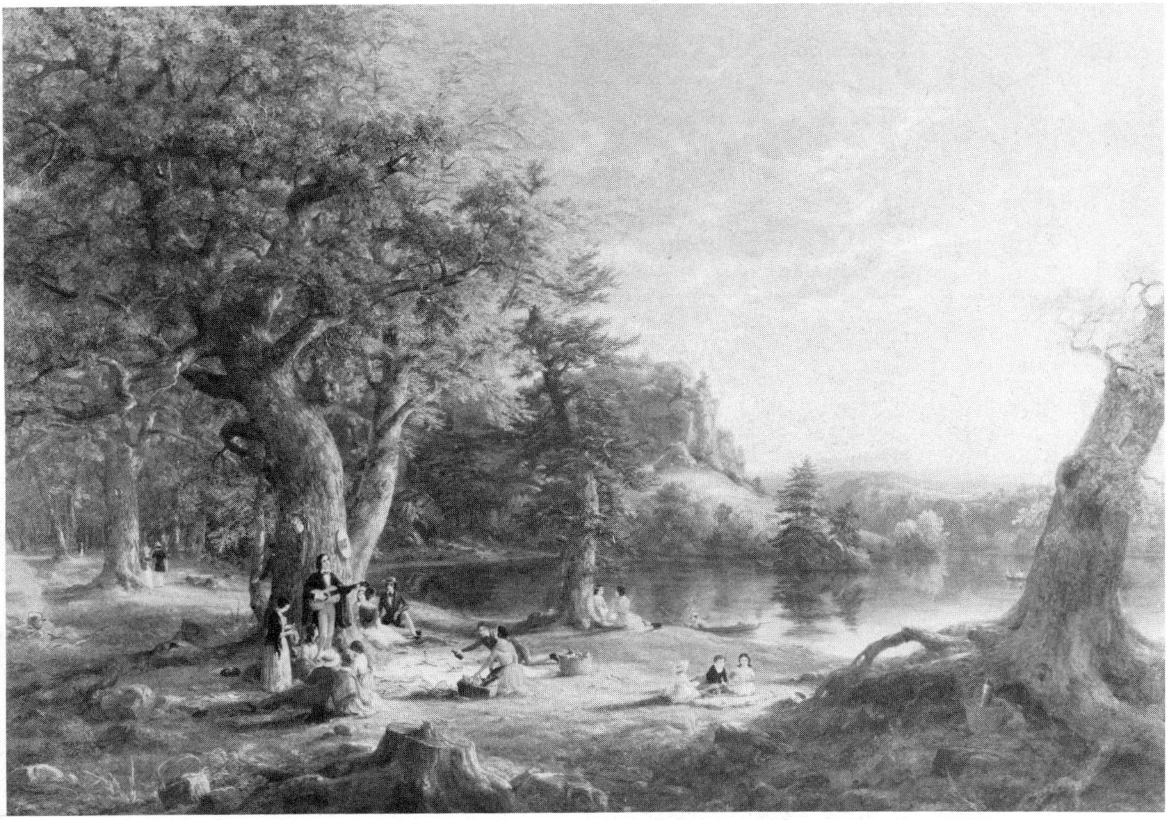

Figure 4-3. *The Pic-Nic,* by Thomas Cole. 1846. Oil on canvas, 44⅞″ × 71⅞″. (Brooklyn Museum, A. Augustus Healy Fund, New York).

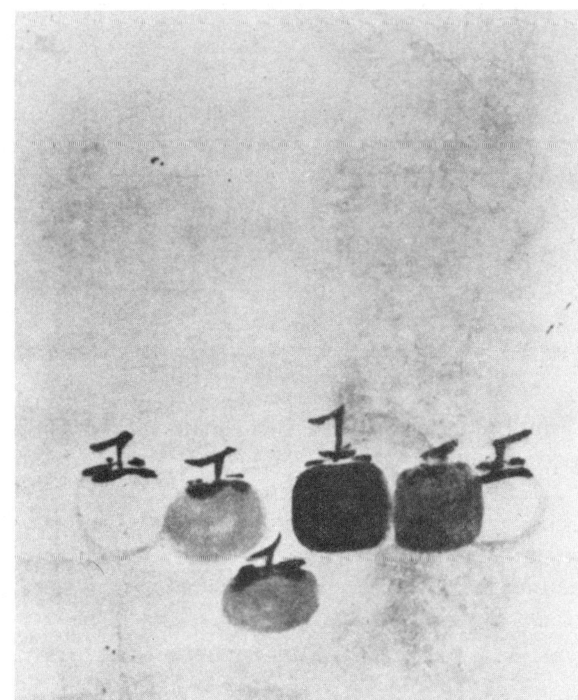

Figure 4-4. *The Six Persimmons,* by Mu Ch'i. 1268. Brush and ink, 14⅛″ × 11¼″. (Ryoko-In, Daito-kuji, Kyoto, Japan).

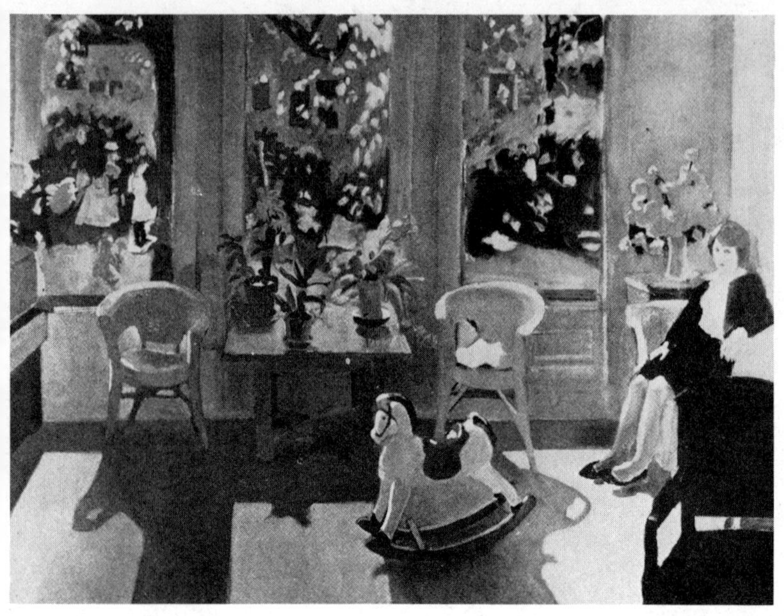

Figure 4-6. *Suprematist Composition: White on White,* by Kasimir Malevich. 1918. Oil, 31¼″ × 31¼″. (Museum of Modern Art, New York).

ized a higher reality than the surface appearance of things (Fig. 4-7). Islamic artists, whose religion prevented them from making images, gradually developed an art in which math and aesthetics became one (Fig. 4-8). Western architecture and engineering are exceedingly rich with similar marriages.

Painters such as Josef Albers were among the courageous visual thinkers of modern Europe who restricted the variables of painting to a minimum of simple

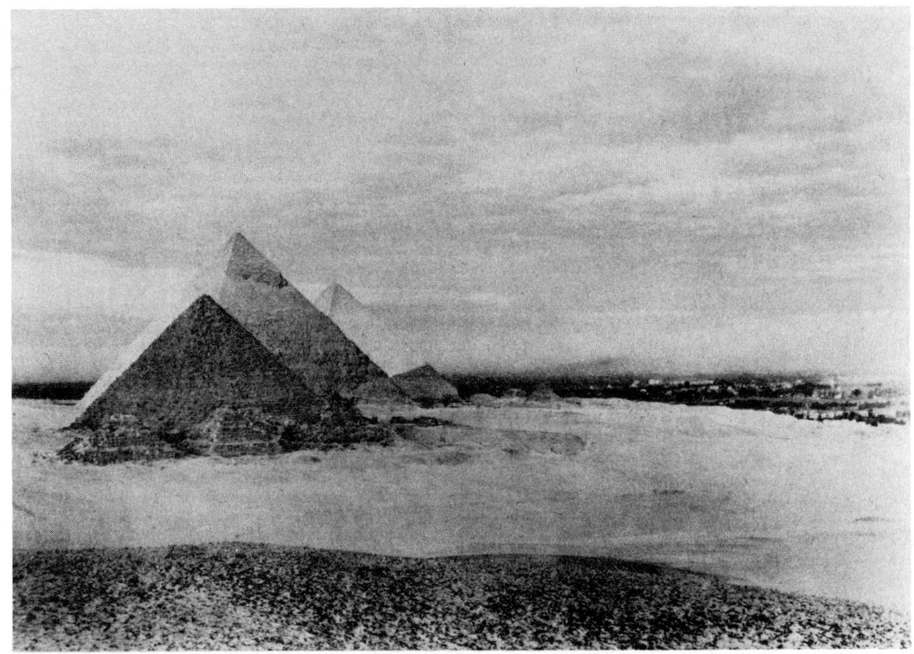

Figure 4-7. The pyramids near Giza, Egypt, are a reminder that geometry has often symbolized a higher reality than the surface appearance of things. Reprinted, with permission, from Geoffrey and Susan Jellicoe, *Landscape of Man* (Thames and Hudson, Ltd., London, 1975).

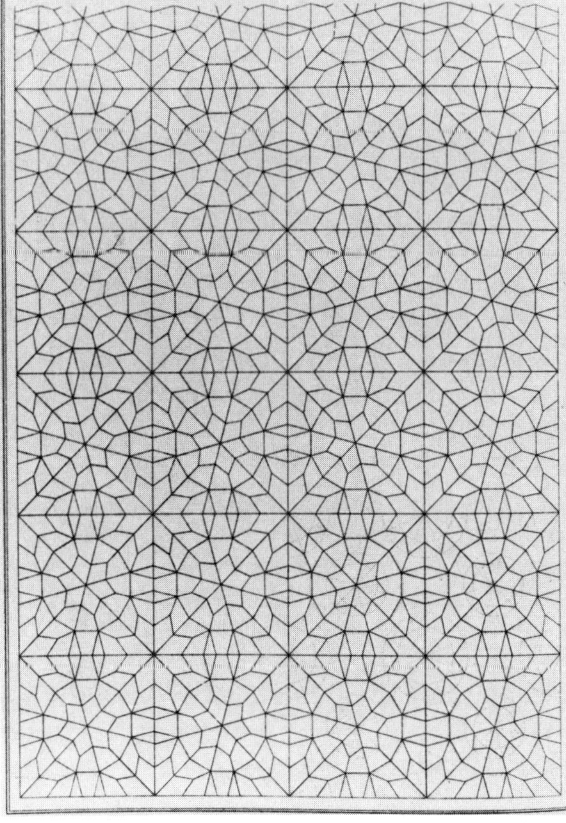

Figure 4-8. Islamic pattern: Math and aesthetics became one in Islamic art. Reprinted, with permission, from J. Bourgoin, *Arabic Geometrical Pattern and Design* (Dover Publications, Inc., New York, 1973).

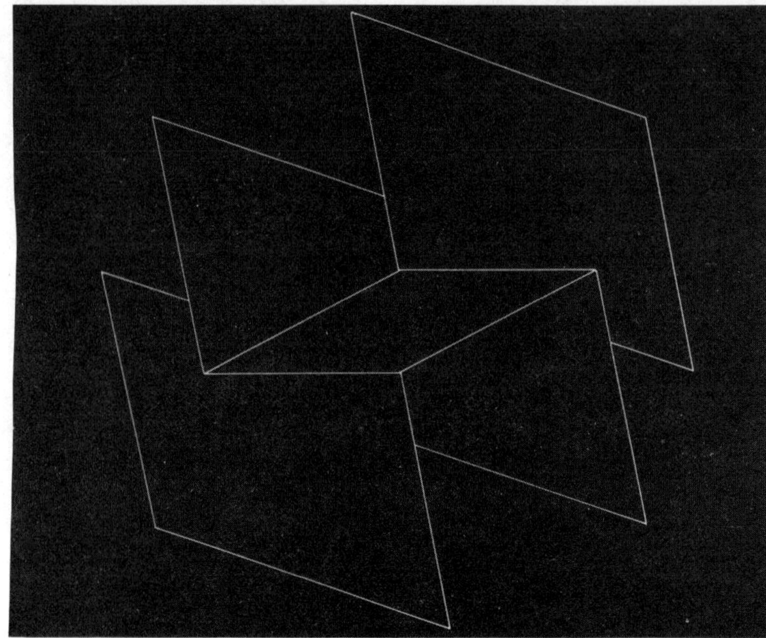

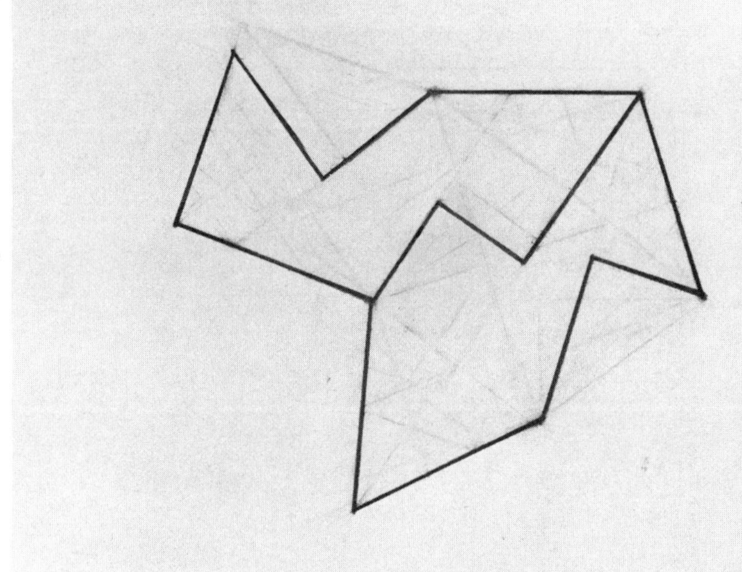

Figure 4-9. *Structural Constellations,* by Josef Albers. 1953–58. Reprinted, with permission, from Francois Bucher, *Despite Straight Lines* (The MIT Press, Cambridge, 1958).

Figure 4-10. *Untitled (Cuts),* by Mel Bochner. 1979. Charcoal on Arches buff paper, 22¼″ × 29⅝″. (Sonnabend Gallery, New York).

forms and colors interacting on a flat plane. No matter how extreme such works may seem to a person just beginning the study of art, an understanding of the revolutionary change of attitude reflected by the underlying principles of the works must be attained before the present visual milieu can be understood (Fig. 4-10).

Placement

I asked each member of a class to write a paragraph about drawing. One of the students wrote, "Drawing leads to an awareness of the physical world—a sensitivity to placement of things in one's surroundings. I constantly want to shift chairs, books, bottles to make a finer pattern where I live."

A choreographer deals with the confines of a stage. Similarly, a visual artist must place forms within a definite space: a page, a canvas, a building site, a museum wall, or an urban space. Architects must have a clear visual conception of their design for a site before they can become deeply involved in further aspects of planning. A building's wall might be likened to canvas on which the forms of windows and doors are placed. This idea can be sensed when looking at Le Corbusier's careful placement of windows on the walls of his chapel at Ronchamp (Fig.

Figure 4-11. Architects must have a clear visual concept of their design for a site before they can become deeply involved in further aspects of planning. Reprinted, with permission, from *Brookhaven College, Campus Master Plan* (Pratt, Box, Henderson & Partners, Dallas).

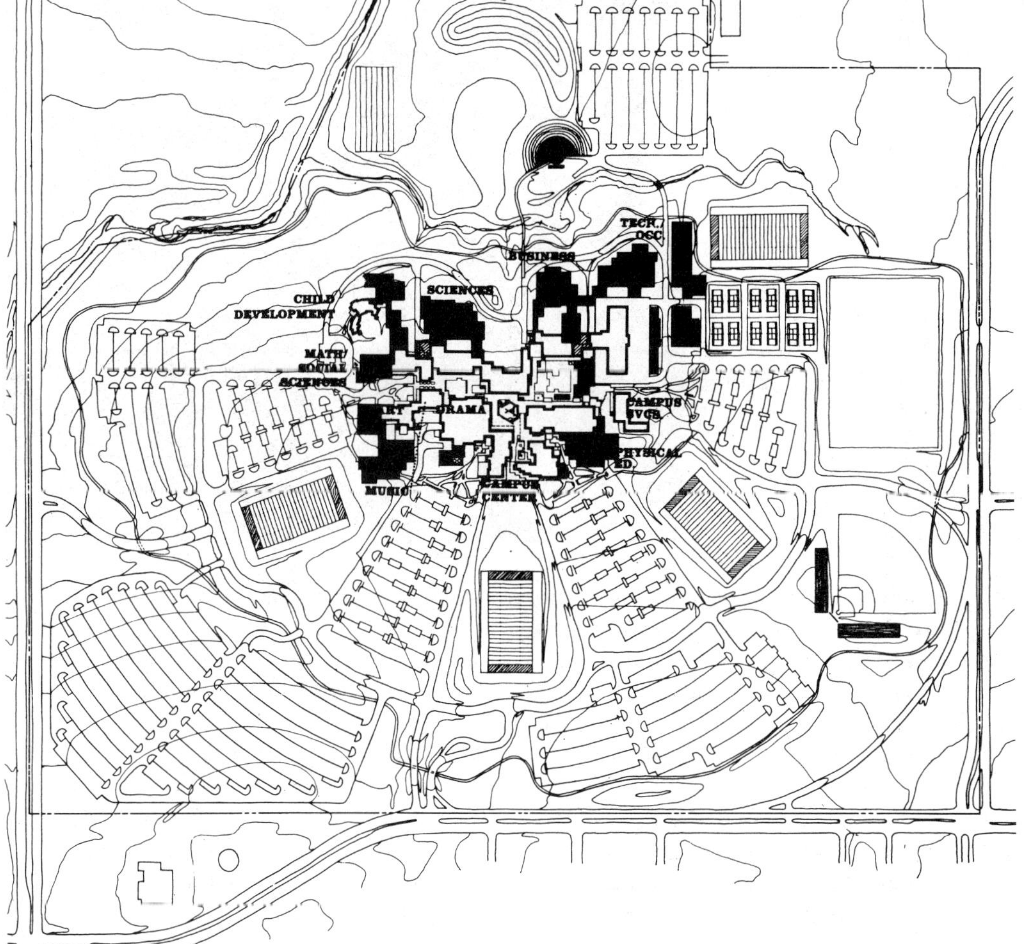

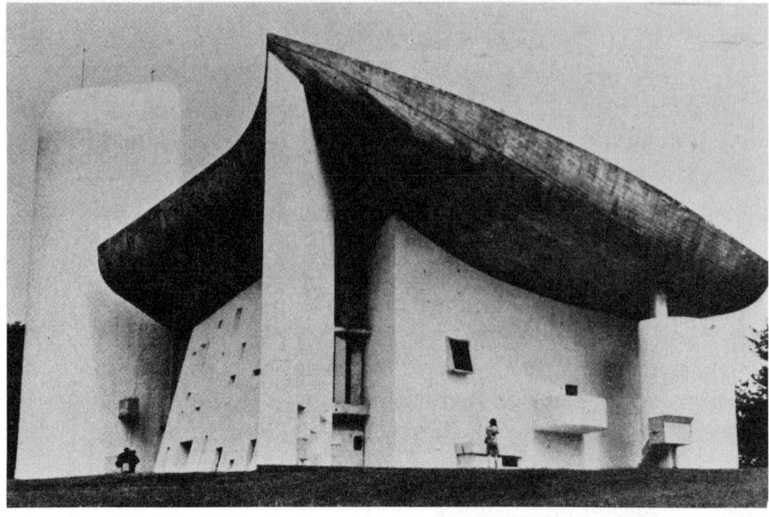

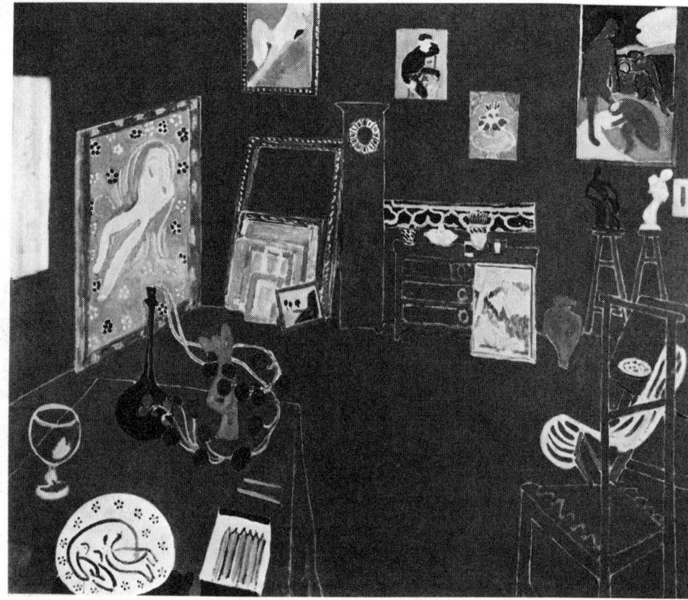

4-12). The cast ferroconcrete forms of the structure itself have been placed against the background planes of earth and sky.

Matisse's *The Red Studio* (Fig. 4-13) gives us a rare insight into how the artist arranged paintings and other objects against the planes of his studio walls and floor, and also how he arranged forms on the surface plane of a canvas. We can learn much from observing the intervals between objects (the negative space), the scale variation from large to small within the intervals and objects, and the play of curves in a predominantly rectilinear environment.

Shape and Texture

Shape has become the most popular forming device in recent art history because its two-dimensional nature lends itself so readily to the retention of the picture plane. Retention of the plane is automatic when pure shape is used (Fig. 4-14). But even when shapes are only implied, as in Fig. 4-15, our attention is held on the surface plane because the interaction of areas bound by lines energizes two-dimensional space while de-emphasizing deep space.

Texture, or the treatment of the surface plane with a repetitive mark or combination of marks, can help retain the picture plane by pulling our attention to

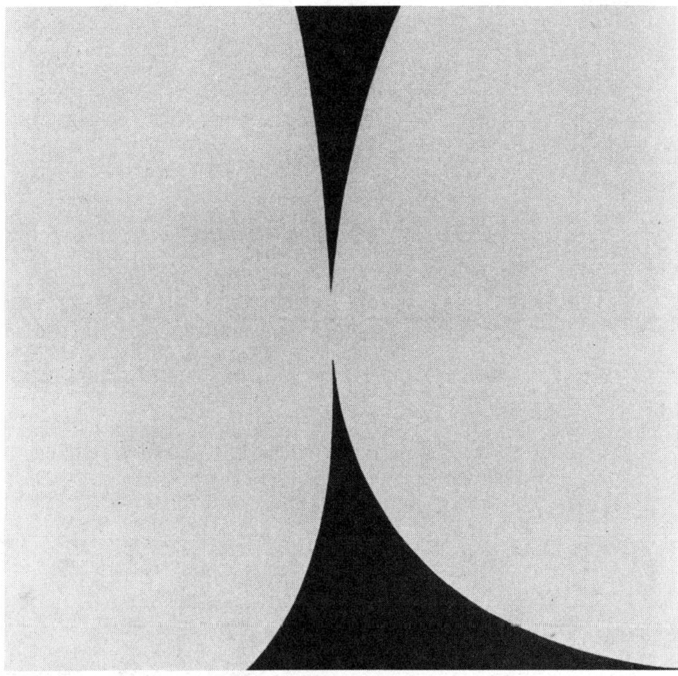

Figure 4-14. Shape facilitates retention of the surface plane. *Rebound,* by Ellsworth Kelly. 1959. Oil on canvas, 68½″ × 71½″. Collection of D. Franklin Könisberg, (Leo Castelli Gallery, New York).

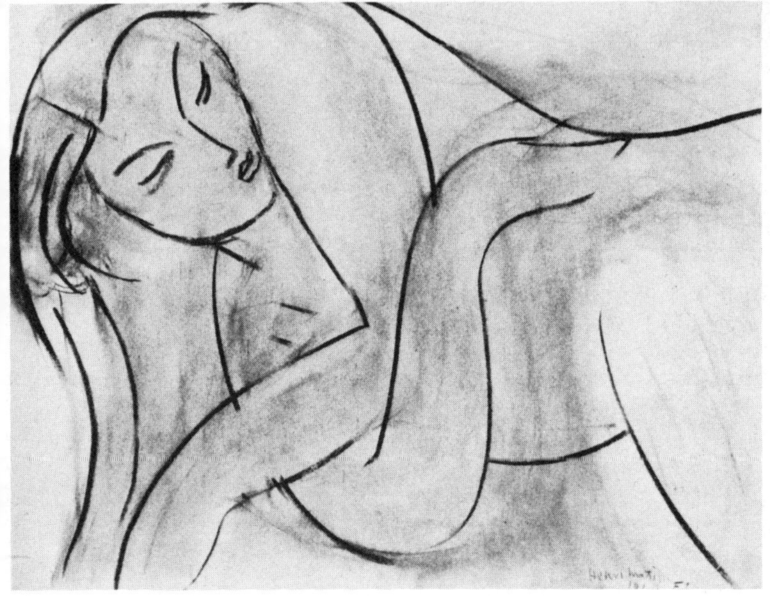

Figure 4-15. *Theme F, Variation 1,* by Henri Matisse. 1941. Charcoal, 15¾″ × 20½″. (Musée de Peinture et de Sculpture, Grenoble, France.)

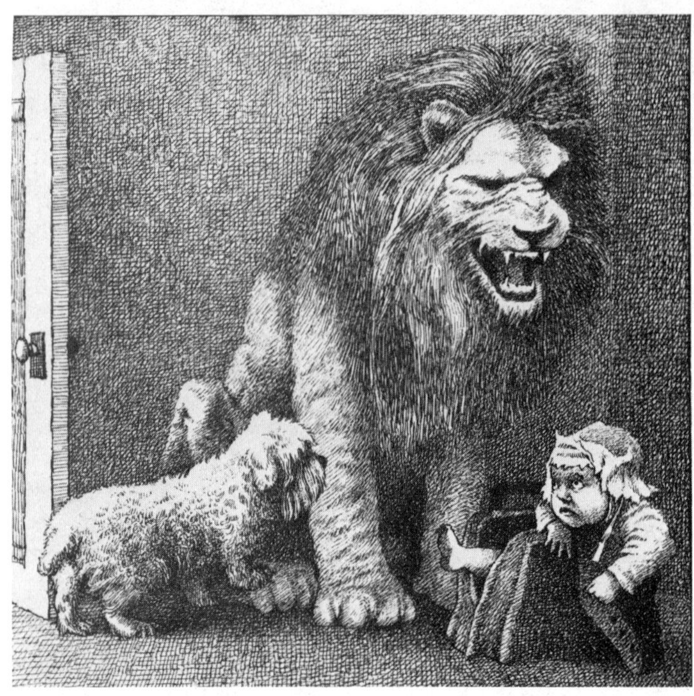

Figure 4-16. Illustration, by Maurice Sendak. Reprinted, with permission, from Maurice Sendak, *Higglety Pigglety Pop! Or There Must Be More to Life* (Harper & Row, Publishers, Inc., New York, 1967).

Figure 4-17. *The Lion Gardiner House, Easthamptom,* by Childe Hassam. 1920. Etching, 9⅞″ × 14″. Reprinted, with permission, from Joseph S. Czestochowski, ed., *Ninety-Four Prints by Childe Hassam* (Dover Publications, Inc., New York, 1980).

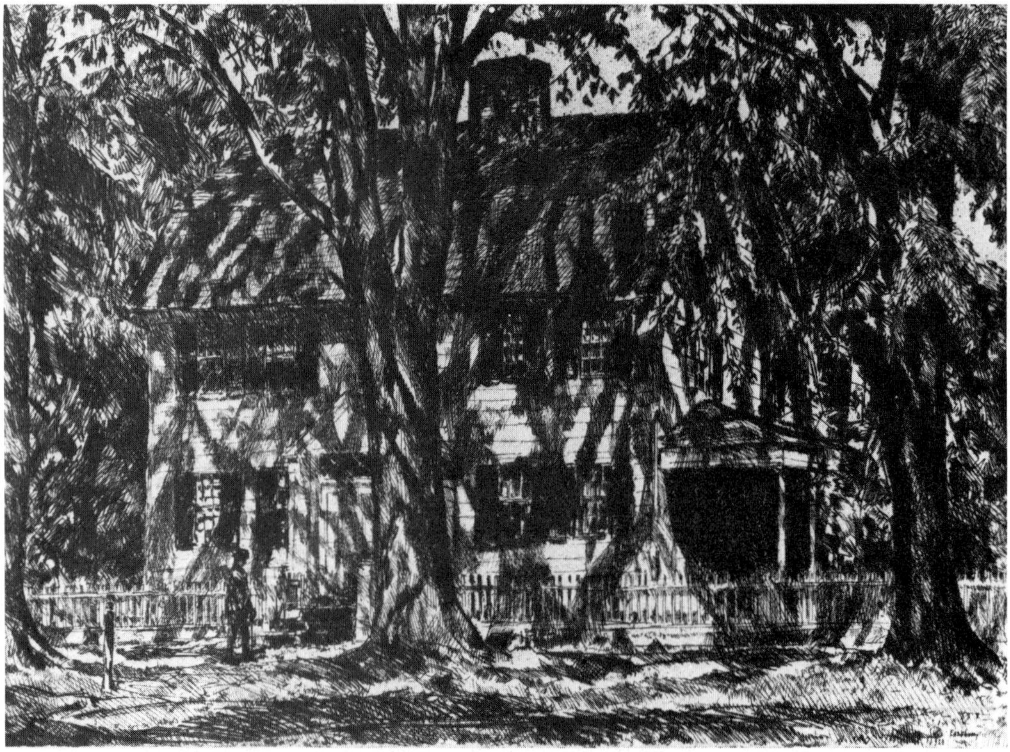

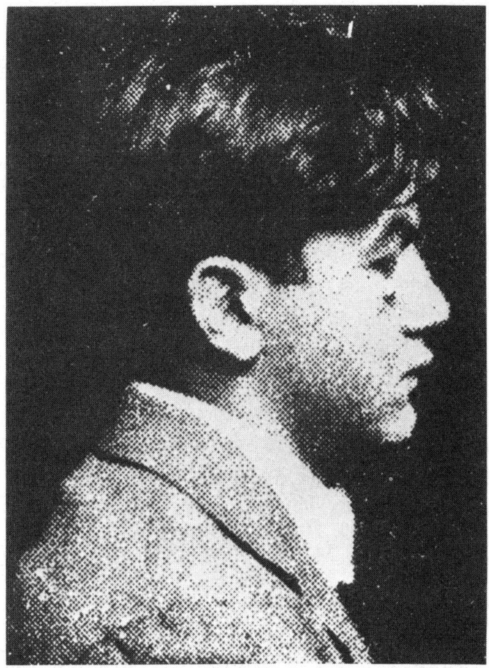

Figure 4-18. *Most Wanted Men No. 2, John Victor G.*, by Andy Warhol. 1963. Silkscreen on canvas, 48″ × 39⅜″. © Andy Warhol, 1982. (SPADEM, Paris/VAGA, New York)

the overall surface. In Figs. 4-16, 4-17, and 4-18 our eyes are attracted again and again to the surfaces by the complexity of visual events, whether they are dots, dashes, squiggles, cross-hatches, or any combination of these typical textural devices. Notice the different types of marks in the little Van Gogh pen-and-ink sketch (Fig. 4-19).

COMPOSING THE PAGE: EXERCISES

In drawing, one should never stop considering the page. Placement, open space, positive-negative relationships, shape,

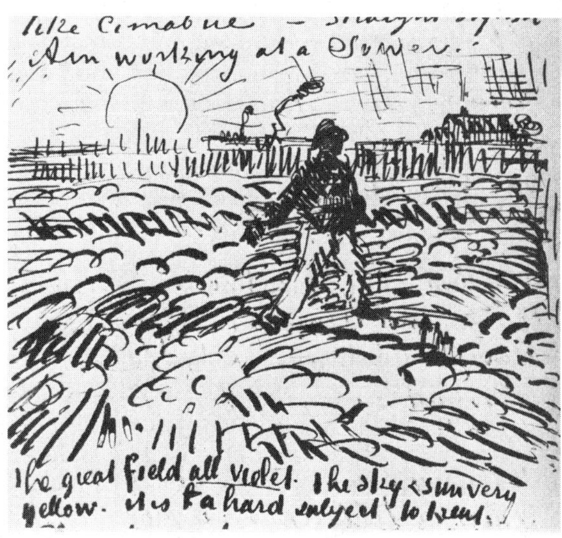

Figure 4-19. Sketch from letter, by Vincent van Gogh. Pen and ink, 7″ × 9½″. (National Museum Vincent van Gogh, Amsterdam).

and texture—these are as important to drawing as to any other form of planning within a frame of reference. An isolated exercise can bring a heightened interest in the page to a student who may have grasped the concepts of dealing with two-dimensional space, but cannot yet put the concepts into material form.

Compositional Studies

In *The Natural Way to Draw*, Nicolaides states unequivocally that students should do six compositional studies of great paintings each day for four years—almost 2,200 studies! Without question, the benefit of such study would be enormous. But even if you subscribed to a less rigorous program of compositional study, you still would profit from discoveries made through the analysis of spatial relationships in successful two-dimensional objects.

All kinds of photographic materials are worthy of study, from art photography to reproductions of paintings and photographs of outstanding examples of architecture and engineering. (The last category would be useful as a method of studying the structure of a building or bridge, but would not be helpful as a study of the division of a rectangular plane, since such photographs are likely to be negligible page compositions.)

When studying from a slide or other reproduction, you should first turn the work upside down or on either side so that the subject or symbolic content is de-emphasized and the structural qualities and other relationships are made more important. Complete the study by turning both the reproduction and your work in each of the other three directions, making changes on your study with each turn. Use long, sweeping lines. Look past surface details to the largest, broadest division of space you can see. Use simple materials for these studies: an ordinary pencil and some newsprint, paper towels, or whatever paper is available.

Always start the study by making a rectangle that closely approximates the proportions of the work being studied. Don't spend more than two or three minutes working in any one direction. *The entire study should take no longer than ten minutes.* Studying a work longer would only increase a beginner's interest in its details, technique, and surface meanings; in other words, all the superficialities that simply lead you away from the essential aims of the exercise—to see and work broadly in order to understand the underlying spatial relationships of the composition being studied. Now and then these studies can be substituted for quick drawings from the model.

This exercise can be developed into a value study by using conté rather than pencil and line. The same process of turning the reproduction and your work in all four directions should be followed. But now you should be finding not only linear

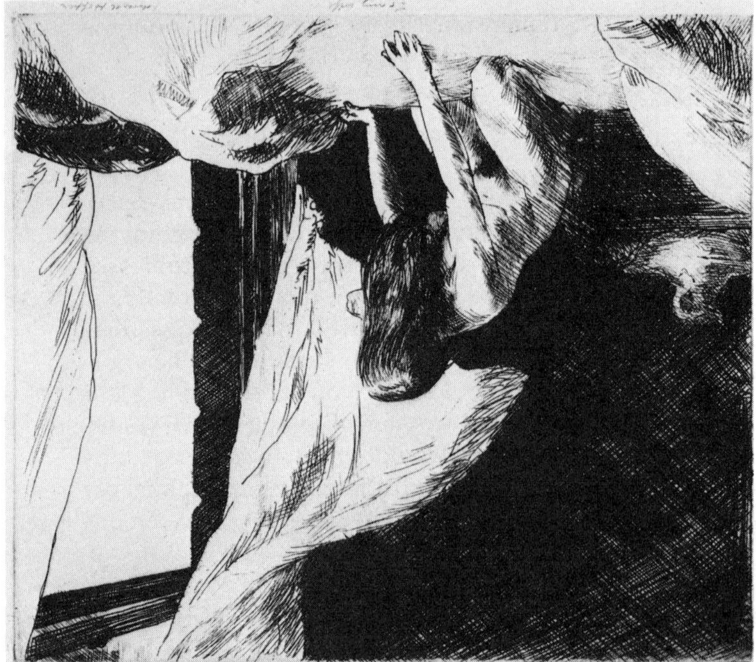

Figure 4-20. Structural relationships are made more important and the subject less important by turning the work upside down. *Evening Wind,* by Edward Hopper (presented upside down). 1921. Etching, 6⅞″ × 8¼″. (Whitney Museum of American Art, New York, bequest of Josephine N. Hopper).

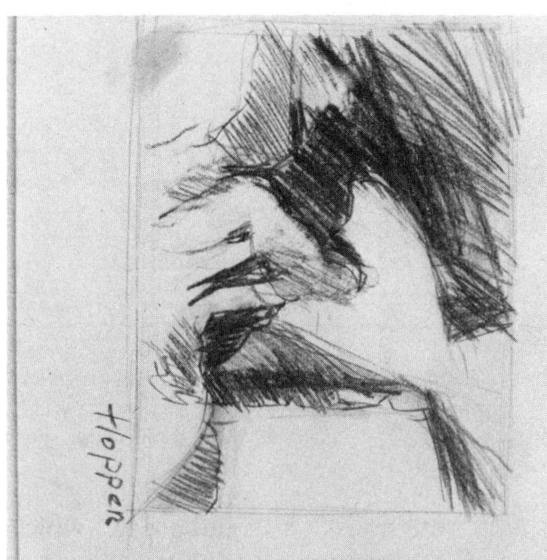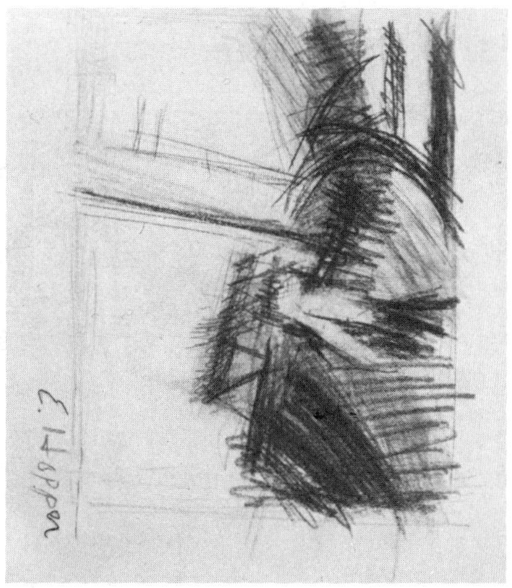

Figure 4-21. Compositional studies of Hopper etchings. *Evening Wind* and *Crossing Railroad*, by Marilu Gruben (art education major). (Jean Mitchel).

divisions of space but also the largest masses of light and dark; the simplest value pattern. Try to limit yourself to three values: light, middle, and dark. These studies, like the ones in pencil, should be done quickly—no more than ten minutes per study—and they, too, can be substituted for quick drawings from the model.

Figure 4-22. *Sketch after Rubens' "Debarkation of Marie de' Medici at Marseilles"*, by Eugene Delacroix. Pencil, 11″ × 10″. (The Louvre, Paris).

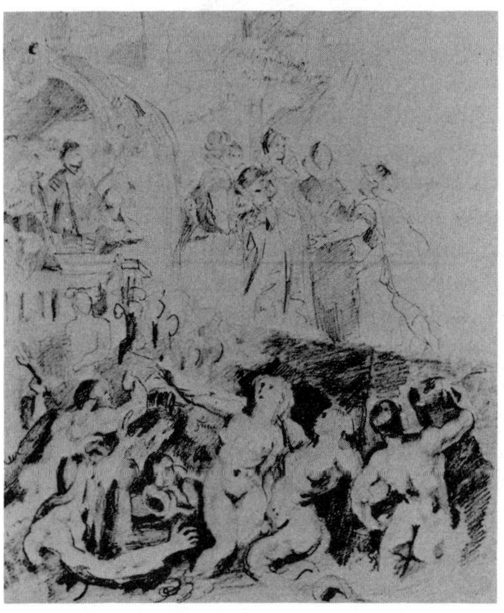

You can make similar compositional studies in collage. A very quick collage study of a composition is shown in Fig. 4-23, and a very elaborate study is shown in Fig. 4-24. This exercise often proves to be especially helpful in loosening up inhibited students and giving them confidence in handling space. Color masses as well as value masses can be used in collage studies. I'll remind you of my suggestion in Chapter 1 that colored paper found in magazines, printed material, wrapping paper, and the like be used rather than purchased packets or sheets of paper, as the latter tend to feel coldly consistent. Corrugated cardboard cut up into appropriate squares is an adequate ground for small compositional studies in collage. White glue, or even rubber cement, and a pair of utility scissors (with the understanding that paper can be torn as well as cut) are all the additional materials you need. You should be rough and free with these studies, never thinking of them as finished products, or objects. If you approach the materials with fear, you will be keeping yourself from

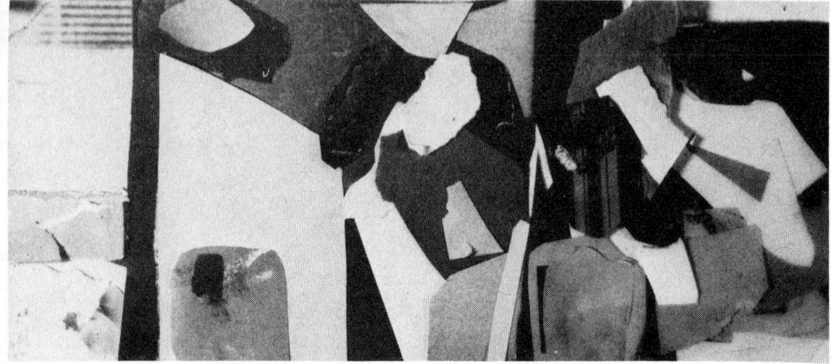

is a roughness, a spontaneity, which keeps the materials and the structure of the work alive. To aid in keeping your own work alive, don't spend more than twenty minutes on any one collage.

Adding Space

Degas often added space to his pastels and other drawings to accommodate his enlarging spatial idea as a work progressed. I suggest that you occasionally imitate Degas in this regard by enlarging the spatial concept of a drawing through taping on additional paper at the top, bottom, or sides of the page. Adding on, like cropping, heightens one's awareness of page space. However, they differ in several important ways. Cropping a drawing inevitably creates a closeup, while adding on gives you more space to deal with. When paper is *added*, a physical means must be found to hold the various pieces together. This process helps to sensitize you to the weight and surface of paper as a material. Also, when paper is added (the same kind as the original drawing or a different kind), one senses the shift to a collage process, making the involvement in drawing more daring and conceptually more exciting. The new edges brought about by the addition of

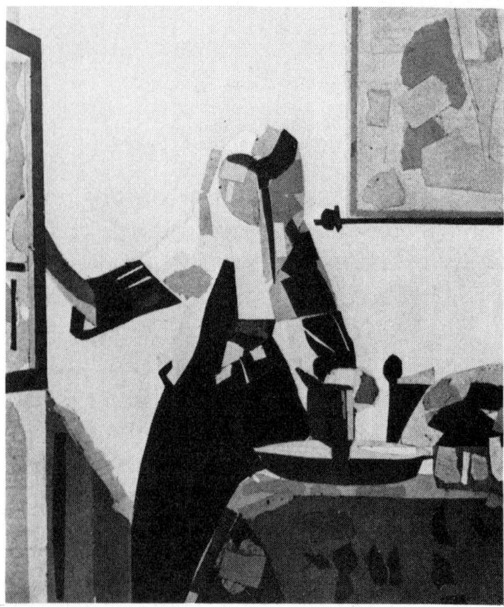

Figure 4-24. Color paper study of Vermeer painting, *Young Woman with a Water Jug*. Reprinted, with permission, from Josef Albers, *The Interaction of Color* (Yale University Press, New Haven, 1963).

learning all that you can learn and doing all that you can do. A friend of mine who teaches clarinet stresses to his students the necessity of learning *forte* before *piano*. The same applies to collage and other methods of drawing. A young artist must learn to be strong before any force can be brought to delicacy. Even in the mature work of Romare Bearden (Fig. 1-12) there

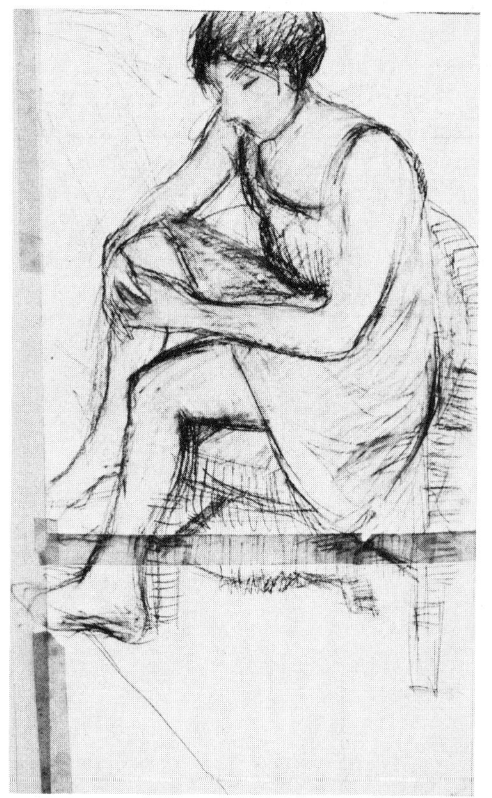

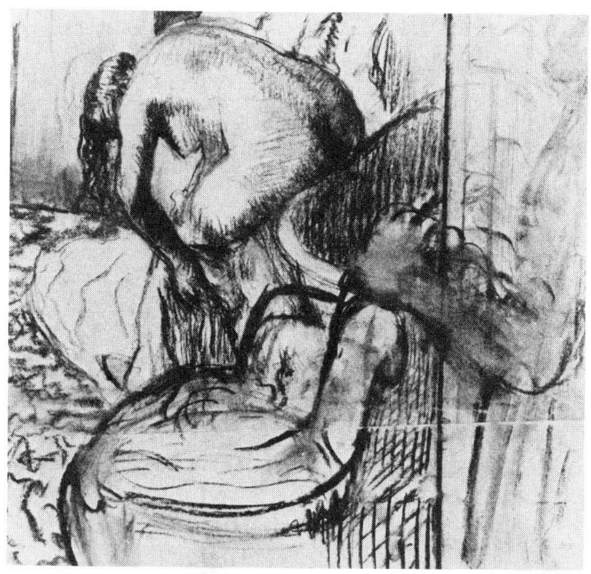

Figure 4-25. The added space at the bottom accommodates Degas' enlarging spatial idea. *After the Bath,* by Edgar Degas. c. 1900. Charcoal and pastel, 22″ × 23¾″. Collection of Ayala Zacks. (City Art Museum of St. Louis, Missouri).

Figures 4-26 and **4-27.** When paper is added, a suitable means must be found to hold the pieces together. Added-on drawings, by Ro Reinthal (art major). (Jean Mitchel).

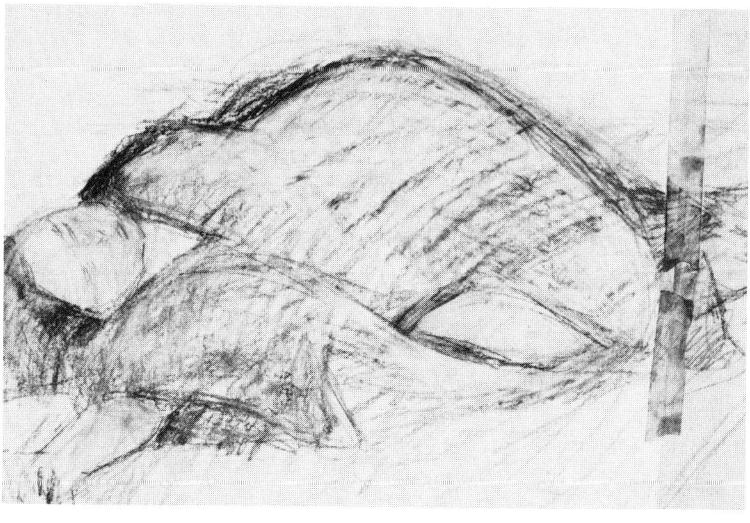

paper become a part of the drawing—a new element—to be worked with as much as a drawn line or any other element in the drawing.

SUMMARY

Open space must interact with any form or image drawn in the space. Modern Western artists have been interested in two-dimensional space and the retention of the surface plane, or picture plane. They have experimented broadly with geometry as a means to bring a painting up to the surface plane.

Shape, texture, and placement are presented as ideas for reducing deep space by increasing interaction on the picture plane.

Exercises in composition are presented as means of heightening awareness and furthering knowledge of the potential of page usage.

Chapter 5
LINE AND MASS

There is no need to create. To create, to improvise, are words that mean nothing. Genius only comes to those who know how to use their eyes and their intelligence. A woman, a mountain, or a horse are formed according to the same principles.

Auguste Rodin

THE BASIC BUILDING BLOCKS

Line and mass are the basic building blocks of drawing. It is through line and mass that we discover gesture, create areas, place, and measure. In the context of this book, lines are the boundaries of shapes, and mass is three-dimensional shape. When line and mass are combined, these two opposed concepts can pursue a single aesthetic goal through inference and the welding power of suggestion. The Matisse drawing (Fig. 5-1) flaunts—celebrates—the differences between the two concepts, and the drawing is held together by the artist's exquisite understanding of the drawing process.

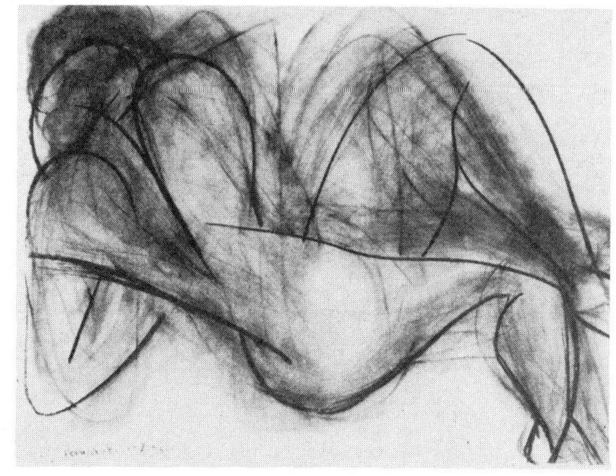

Figure 5-1. *Reclining Nude Seen From the Back,* by Henri Matisse. 1938. Charcoal on paper, 23⅝″ × 31⅞″. (Baltimore Museum of Art).

Notice how the drawing reveals its own evolution, making change a part of the product.

LINE

Although lines can be thought of in terms of stylistic treatment, or as formal elements with intrinsic properties, the only purpose for lines in the present context is to divide one area from another, leaving positive and negative areas with equal strength. To match this purpose your line quality should be even and consistent— no variations for aesthetic purposes. For the successful use of this line you need an acquired or natural sensitivity to the interaction of positive and negative areas. If you only consider the positive shape, the line will imprison the shape rather than letting it interrelate with its negative surroundings on an equal basis. If you only consider the negative shape, the positive shape will be lifeless.

Potted plants are perfect subjects for line studies. Their natural grace brings pleasure to the process of drawing them. The presence of potted plants gives the drawing room environment an interest-ing new dimension in terms of shape and line. The following line study of a potted plant is apt to be so painless that ending the session may be difficult.

For your first line study you will need an 18″ × 24″ sheet of newsprint or all-purpose paper clamped to a masonite panel, a No. 2B drawing pencil (a regular writing pencil will do), and a standard eraser. Choose a simple plant for your subject, and place it on a table near your easel. *Very lightly*, draw in the desired placement of the plant's forms. Placing is not something to be raced through so that you can get on to the ''real'' drawing. Placing is an essential part of the ultimate drawing. Use as much time as you need. Be patient. Only when you feel that you have placed the object as well as you can should you start to draw the specific shapes and movements. Start at any point you wish. Go slowly. Give each area of the drawing an equal amount of time. Take your time and enjoy the proc-ess of discovering the relationships of the shapes.

When drawing one side of a leaf (or one side of a plant), you should fre-quently compare it with the opposite side. Look for rhythm, movement, and

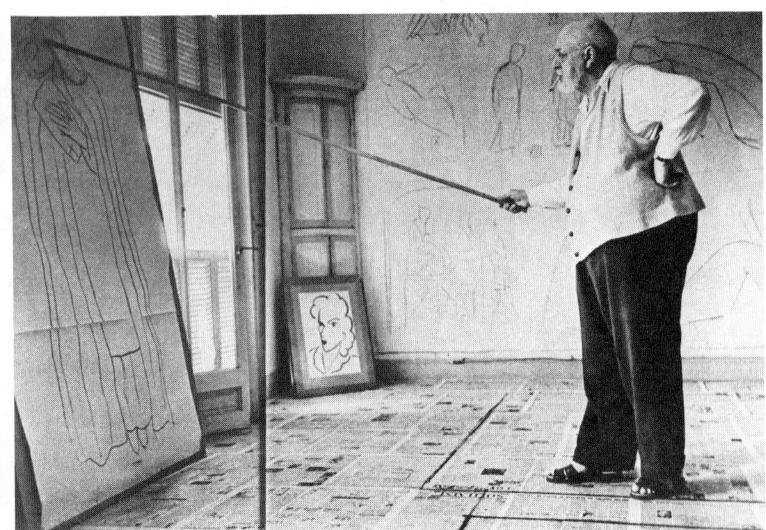

Figure 5-2. Henri Matisse draw-ing with a bamboo pole tipped with charcoal. (Robert Capa/Magnum).

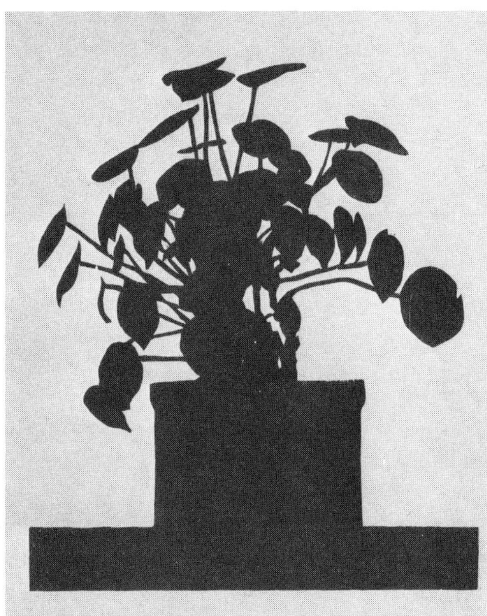

Figure 5-3. The natural grace of potted plants makes studying them a pleasure. *Pepperonia*, by Larry Scholder. 1969. Woodcut, 17½″ × 14″. Collection of the artist. (Larry Scholder).

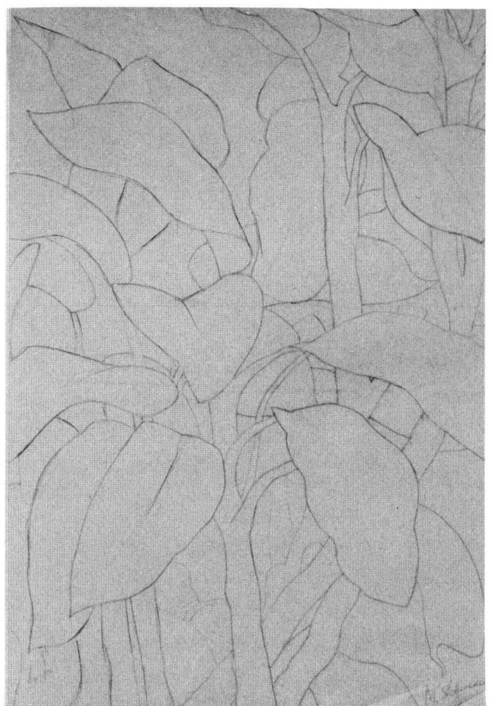

Figure 5-4. Give each area of the drawing an equal amount of time. Line drawing of a plant, by Michael Schroeder (math major). (Jean Mitchel).

asymmetry of form. These give energy to the plant and to your drawing. Don't generalize too much. Look for the subtle details.

Consider the line weight in relation to the page. A heavy line might call too much attention to itself, obliterating the sense of shape. Each line should give a sense of dividing shape from shape—its weight should suit this function and only this function. You may spend as long as two to three hours on this drawing, depending on the complexity of the plant. A subsequent line drawing of a plant (or group of plants with contrasting foliage) might include a model (Fig. 5-5), nude or clothed, in relation to the plants. Approach the model in the same objective spirit as you do the plants.

For quick studies in line you can use scissors rather than pencil. Ask the model to run through a series of five-minute poses with plenty of diagonal movement. Face the model with a piece of newsprint in one hand and a pair of scissors in the other, and start to cut out the shape of the pose. Remember to look for the movement that gives a sense of life to the pose, and try to convey this movement in the shapes you are making. You should not worry about proportions in this exercise. Think more of the gesture—the sense of energy—in the shapes. These are studies that you should feel perfectly free to discard after looking through them and keeping one or two as a record. Cut at least six or seven studies in a session so that you won't think too much about the

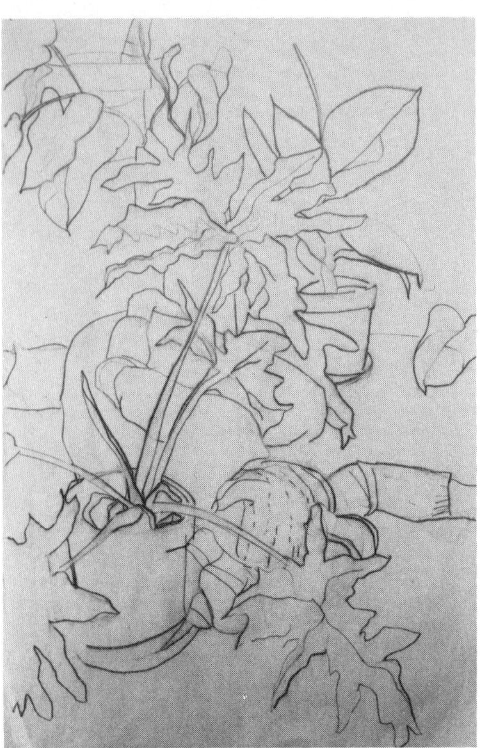

Figure 5-5. Approach the model and the plants in the same objective spirit. Line drawing of a plant and figure, by Joan Blakemore (art education major). (Jean Mitchel).

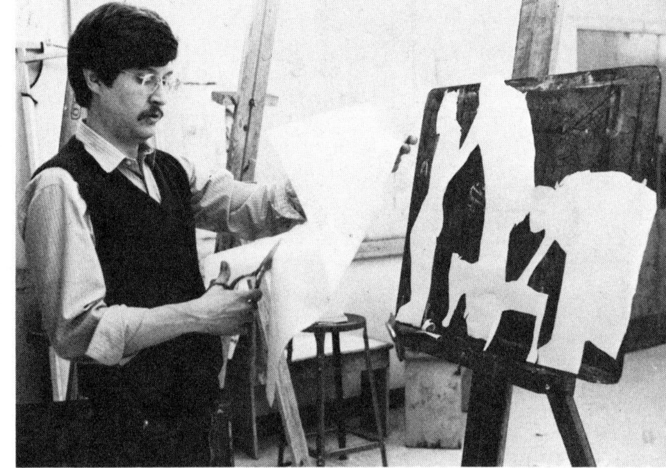

Figure 5-6. Scott Amis (architecture major) cuts a quick study from newsprint. (Jean Mitchel).

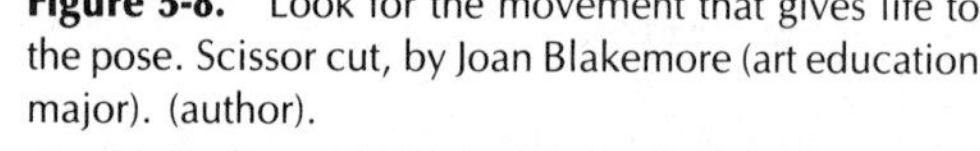

Figure 5-8. Look for the movement that gives life to the pose. Scissor cut, by Joan Blakemore (art education major). (author).

Figure 5-7. Scissor cut, by Margaret Brinson (art education major). (author).

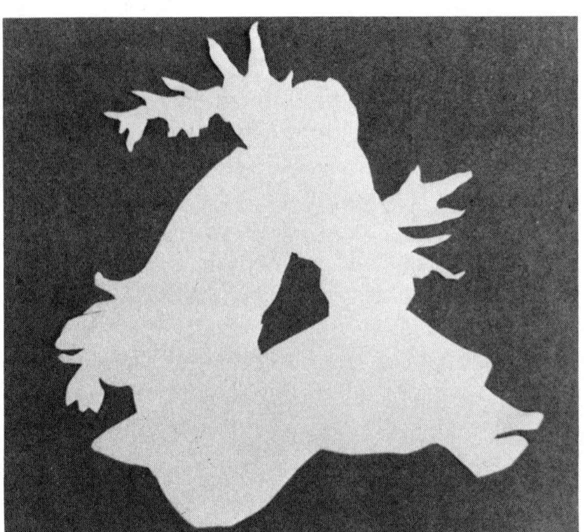

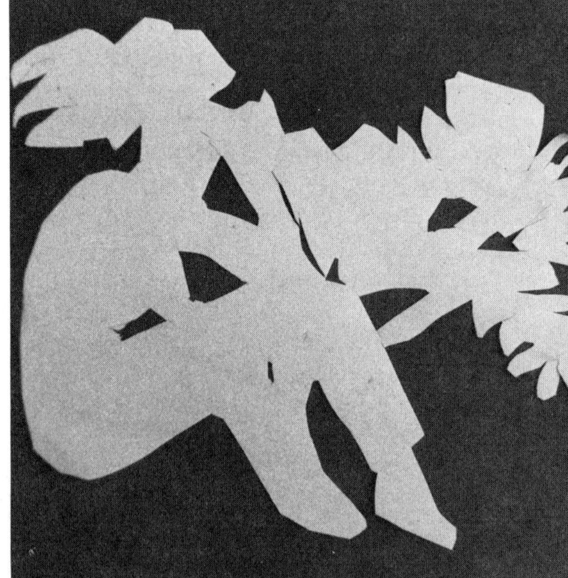

success or failure of a single work. Think about the rhythm; think about the process. Ironically, this approach will produce finer products, since concentration on the process determines the outcome. If you think only of the product, your work is likely to turn out stiff and uninteresting.

For variation, try scissor cuts of potted plants or plants combined with a model.

MASS

Mass is three-dimensional shape. It has volume, air, and light. It exists from front to back as well as from left to right and bottom to top. While using line, you had to think in shape; in two-dimensionality. But now, with mass, you must think of the page as having a potential third dimension in which to move. Mass moves within space.

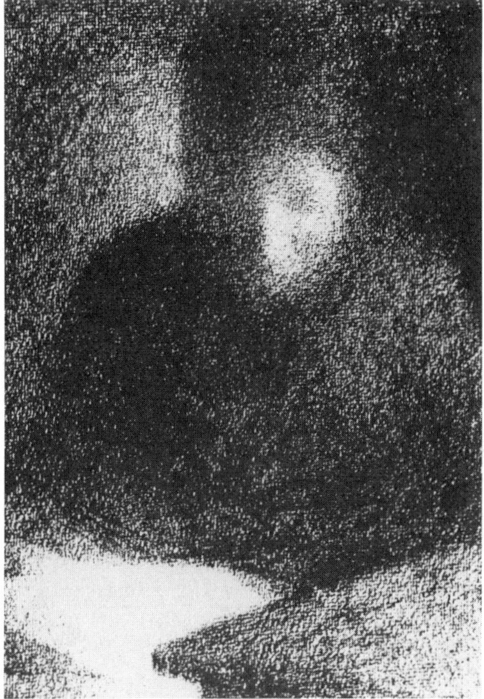

Figure 5-10. Mass does not require lines. *Woman Reading*, by Georges Seurat. Conté crayon, 12½″ × 9″. Reprinted, with permission, from Gustave Kahn, *The Drawings of Seurat* (Dover Publications, Inc., New York, 1971.)

Figure 5-9. Mass moves within space. *La Toilette (Le Bain)*, by Edgar Degas. 1880–85. Monotype in black ink on paper, 12⅜″ × 11″. (Clarence Buckingham Collection, Art Institute of Chicago).

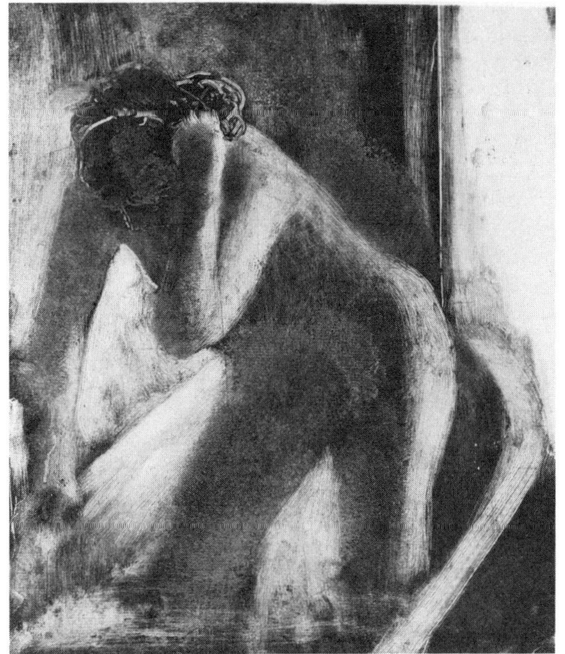

Conté, chamois, kneaded eraser, and newsprint are perfect materials for building a drawing with masses. Mass does not require lines, so your studies should be lineless (Fig. 5-10).

To get started, ask the model to take a series of fifteen- to twenty-minute poses. The model should be in side light so that his or her forms show a very definite light side and dark side. When the model is positioned in the first pose and you have arranged yourself and your easel in proper relation to the model (see Chapter 2), you should start the drawing by looking for the simplest pattern of values; first recording the pattern with the side of the

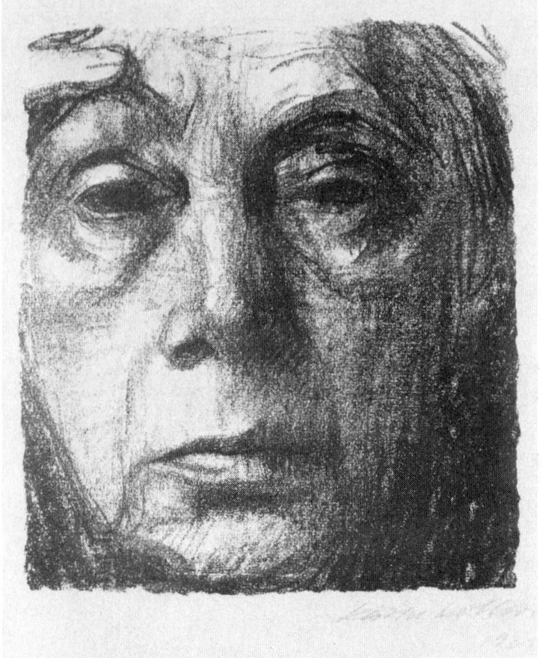

Figure 5-11. *Self Portrait,* by Käethe Kollwitz. 1934. Lithograph, 8⅛″ × 7⅜″. (Philadelphia Museum of Art, given by Dr. and Mrs. William Wolgin).

Clay studies are the most appropriate quick study related to mass (see Chapter 3). The real quality of three dimensions in the clay work forces home an understanding of the positive/negative volume of the model in a room.

Another good mass-related quick approach is to draw with a dirty chamois cloth. The chamois, which should by this point be practically black with conté, becomes an independent drawing tool. The chamois is allowed to follow the movement of the model, as in all one-minute drawing. The details of the forms are ignored. Your search is for the overall; for unity. You won't be able to see the final drawing too well, which may be somewhat frustrating at first, but that is what

Figure 5-12. You can draw with the eraser. Mass study by Marilu Gruben (art education major). (Jean Mitchel).

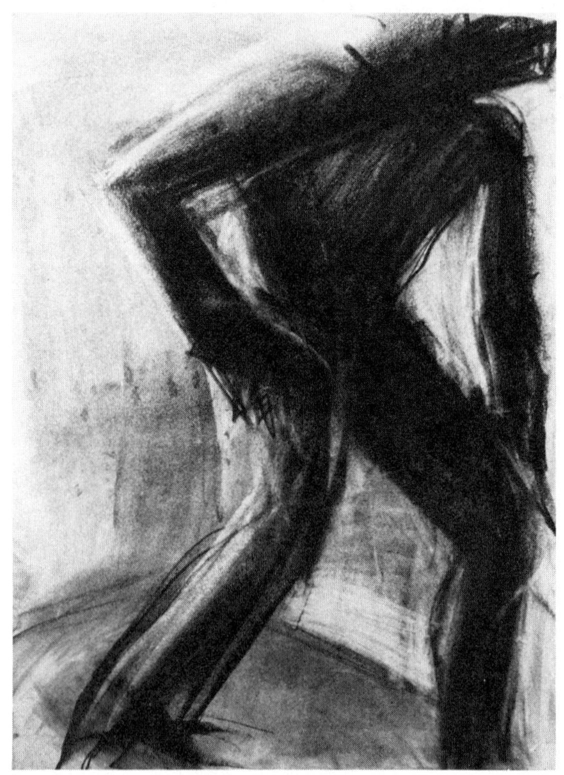

conté and later by rubbing with a chamois cloth and taking tone away with a kneaded eraser. (Keep in mind throughout the process that you can *draw* with the eraser.) Fill up the page. Don't get into specifics. Try for an overall feeling of light and dark masses moving inside a three-dimensional space—a negative volume. If you are able to see only two values on the model, you will be better off. If you see too many values it will be difficult to discern a simple pattern. Squinting at the model helps eliminate excessive information, including too many nuances of light and dark.

To vary the approach with chamois and the crayon's edges, try building up the mass with a series of lines, as in Fig. 5-13. A linear approach to mass will give a clarity to your studies and extend your understanding of the potential of conté.

56

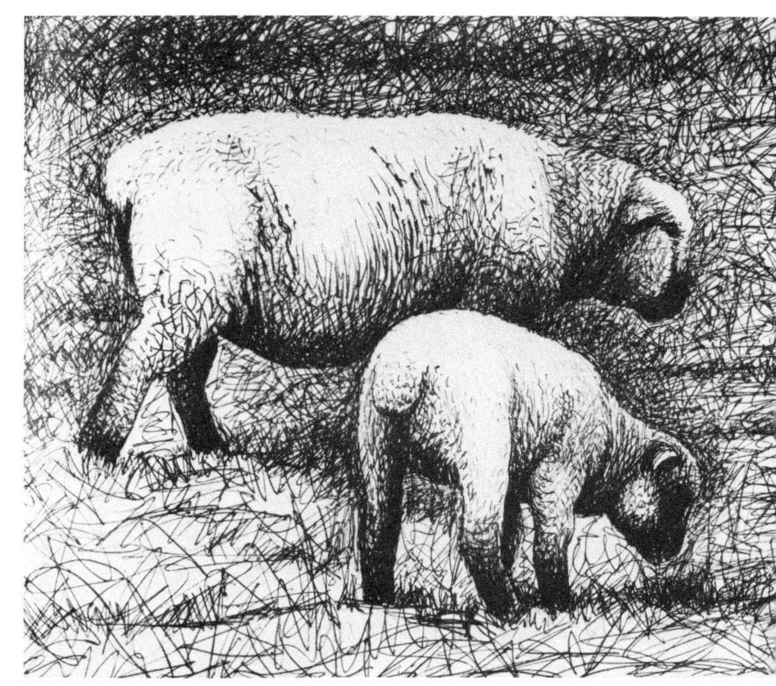

Figure 5-13. A linear approach to mass gives clarity. From *Henry Moore's Sheep Sketchbook,* by Henry Moore and Kenneth Clark (Thames and Hudson, Ltd., London, 1980).

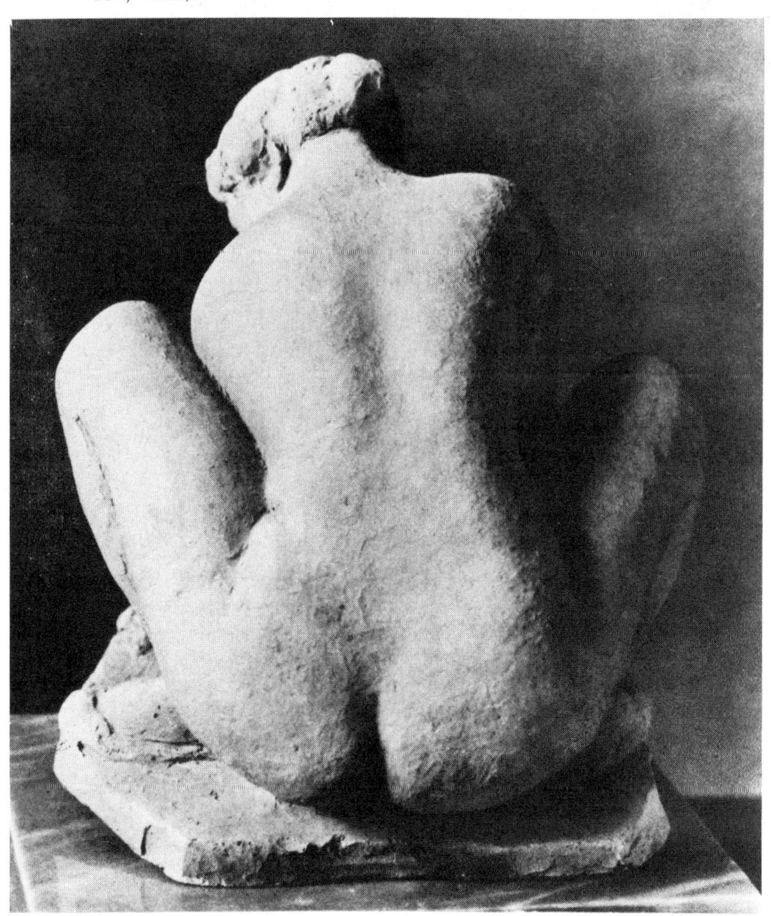

Figure 5-14. Positive/negative volume relationships are learned through clay work. *Woman With a Crab* (back view), by Aristide Maillol. 1930. Clay, 6″ × 4¾″. Courtesy of Galerie Dina Vierny. (© SPADEM, Paris/VAGA, New York, 1982).

57

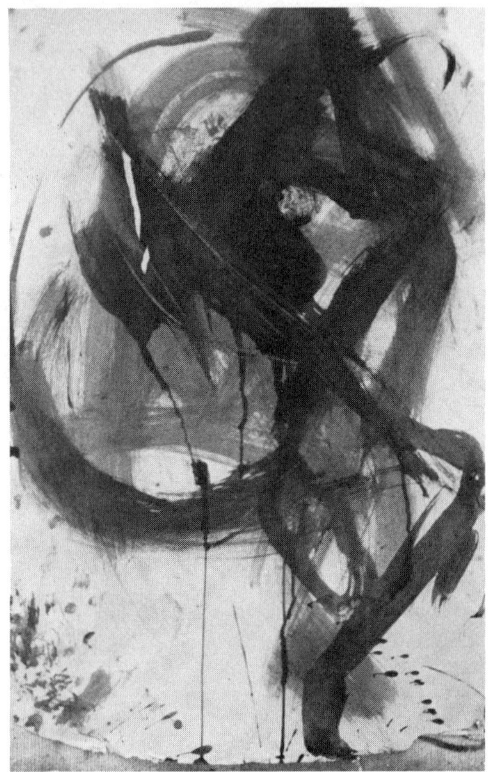

Figure 5-15. Brush and ink drawing, by Mary Elizabeth Howard (art major). (author).

makes this exercise one of the freest and least product-oriented of any in this book.

The medium of brush and ink, as described in Chapter 3, is easily adapted to mass, and you may want to use this medium along with the other quick-study approaches mentioned above.

THE SUSTAINED STUDY IN LINE AND MASS

When mass and line are combined, both are vital elements in the drawing process *from the very start*. To make a line drawing and then fill in with masses, or to make masses and then draw lines around them, would be as inhibiting as a coloring book, and just as mechanical. Masses and lines must be used in *counterpoint*—to borrow a phrase from music—each a part of the original conception and *together* creating a harmonious whole. Don't forgo this principle. Understand it and put it into practice from the start.

A sustained study in line and mass will take at least two hours; longer as your abilities grow. Choose a pose that the model will be able to hold for at least two hours with intermittent breaks. If the pose is a difficult one the model should be given a break every twenty to twenty-five minutes. A simple pose may be held as long as forty-five to fifty minutes without a rest. Experienced models will not take impossible or extremely uncomfortable poses because they know it will prove painful to them and frustrating to the class. As soon as the pose is established, choose a piece of paper of a size, shape, and quality that fits the nature of the exercise and the pose. In other words, choose a paper more substantial than newsprint so that it will stand up under the rough treatment it is about to receive; choose a large enough size to allow you freedom of movement; and choose a shape that fits the composition that the pose suggests.

Start the drawing, as with your first value drawing, by putting a wash of conté over the page, only this time not over the entire page—just roughly over most of it to suggest the weight of the figure and a sense of atmosphere in a room environment. Next, with rough light lines try to show where the main forms of the figure and the main lines of the environment will be. Remember, spend plenty of time with this stage of the drawing—

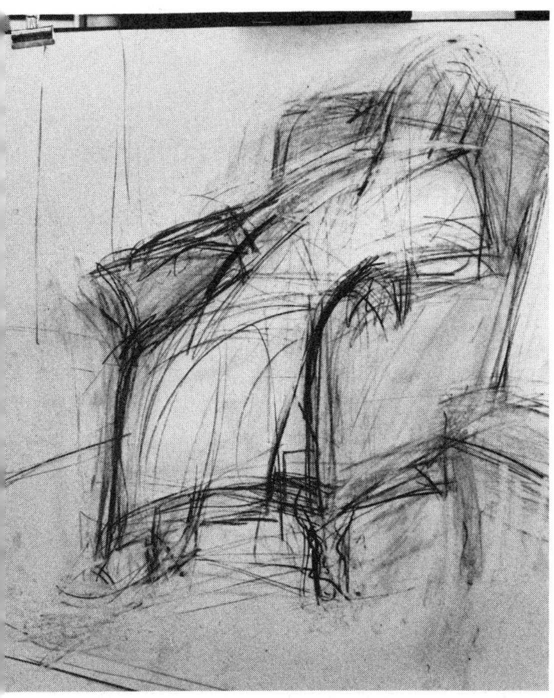

Figure 5-16. Mass and line must be vital elements from the start. Early stage of mass and line study, by Mary Elizabeth Howard (art major). (Lynn Martin).

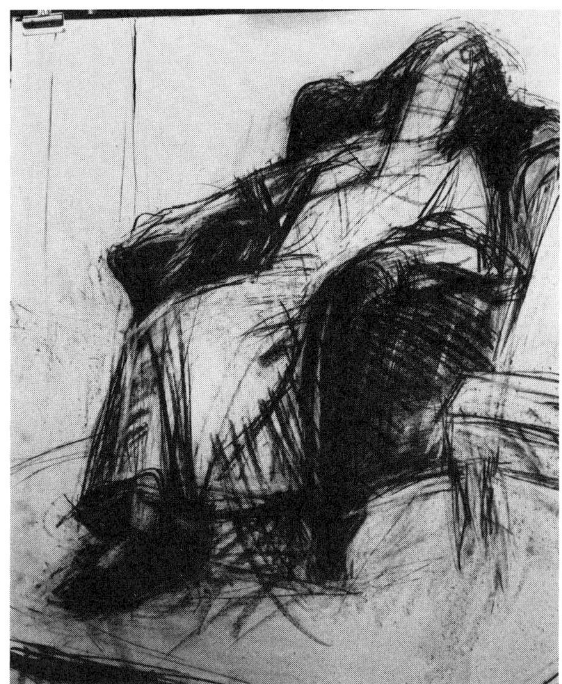

Figure 5-17. Let the drawing breathe. Middle stage of mass and line study, by Mary Elizabeth Howard (art major). (Lynn Martin).

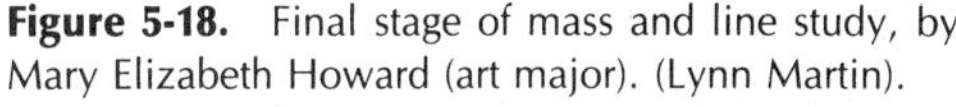

Figure 5-18. Final stage of mass and line study, by Mary Elizabeth Howard (art major). (Lynn Martin).

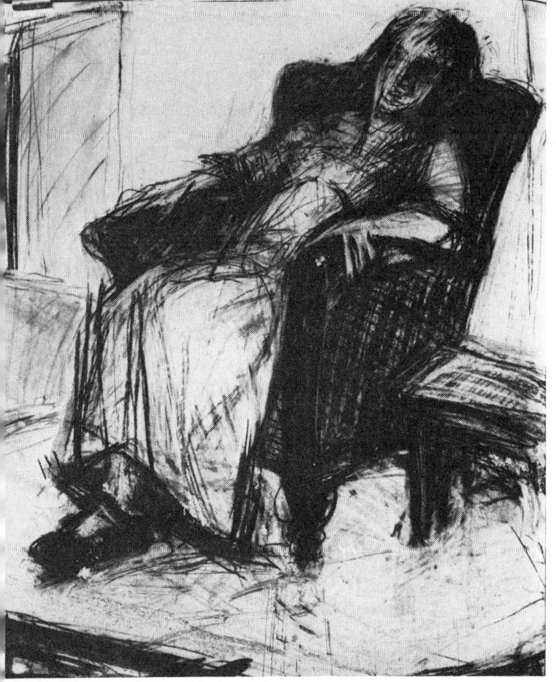

placement is a vital aspect of drawing. Keep the lines light and free to assure that subsequent changes can be made easily. Any hard, heavy lines at this point can make changes next to impossible. Be noncommittal at this stage of the drawing. Let it breathe, just as you do in the quick studies.

After you have established a general placement that satisfies you, and after you have worked out the most general proportions, start to look for a simple value pattern, reinforcing an edge now and then with a line, or using lines that are axial, compositional, or diagrammatic rather than outlines (Fig. 5-19). Lines are notoriously apt to trap errors into your work at this point, so *use them with caution. Let masses lead the way* not only in composition but also in searching for the model's structure and weight.

Feel free to use the conté in as many

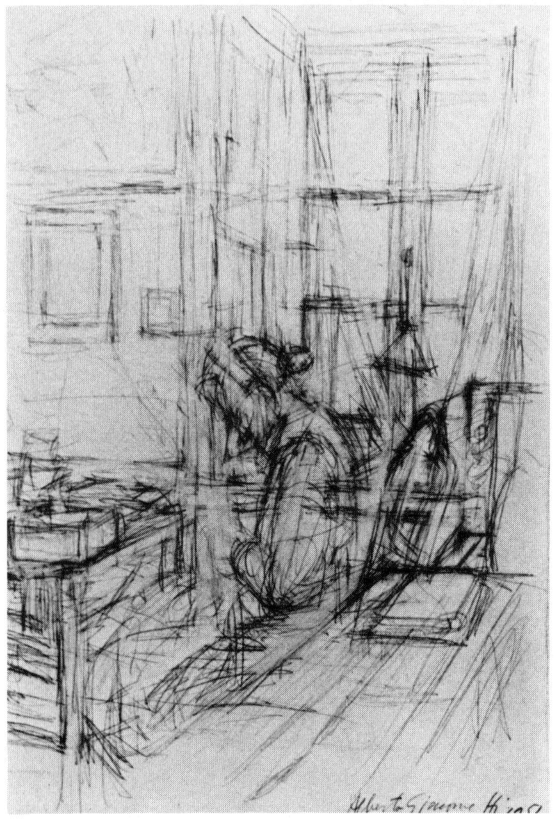

Figure 5-19. Learn to use lines that are axial, compositional, or diagrammatic. rather than outlines. *The Artist's Mother Sewing*, by Alberto Giacometti. 1951. Pencil on cream paper, 14½″ × 10¼″. Collection of Walter Klein. (New York Graphic Society, Ltd., Greenwich).

ways as you can think of. Use its point as well as its edge. Apply it directly; rub it; erase it. A combination of approaches produces a rich sensation of space, richer than a single approach can give. You can draw directly over rubbed or erased areas, and then rub out the direct work and repeat the process (Fig. 5-11). Line as well as mass can be raw or worked. No part of the drawing should be considered final until the process is over. If you commit yourself too early you will find that you are drawing in pieces and trying to protect precious passages.

To the question, "What am I looking for in the sustained study?" I answer that you are looking for a finer and finer abstract quality, or quality of form. Of course, for the drawing to have any authority as a drawing from life, the proportions must be well observed and the volume in space must be strongly communicated. But the ultimate success or failure of the study depends on such considerations as the strength of the structure, the interest of the pattern, and the sense of space, light, and air. Perception and form must work together in balance, but formal considerations must lead the way. The drawing that discourages the drawer is the one obsessed with details, always at the expense of the composition and general force of the total drawing. A student of drawing must learn to generalize, to move away from the specifics of materialistic nature to the broad, simple, general language of form.

The structural principle involved in making a drawing is roughly equivalent to the nature of the formation of mineral crystals. Just as the largest quartz crystal, for instance, is shaped precisely like the smallest quartz crystal, so the largest, broadest aspect of drawing must belong to the same structural system as the smallest detail, despite any shifts and juggling of the form made during the process of the drawing. The drawing, while it maintains its general statement about the model and the environment, moves toward a complete structural study in which all the components are integrated.

Surely all creative activities share to some degree the same process as making a sustained study in line and mass. The first phase is to get one's thoughts down in some form, no matter how rough or out of focus. Then it becomes a matter of going through the rough work, looking for the ideas that are there and those that

Figure 5-20. In drawing from life, the proportions must be well observed and the volume in space must be strongly communicated. Drawing, by Brian Cobble (art major). (Jean Mitchel).

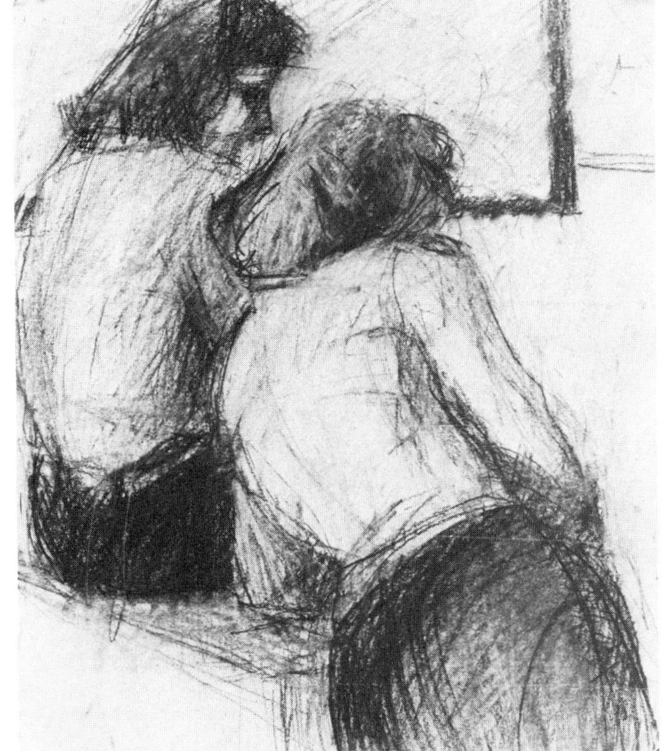

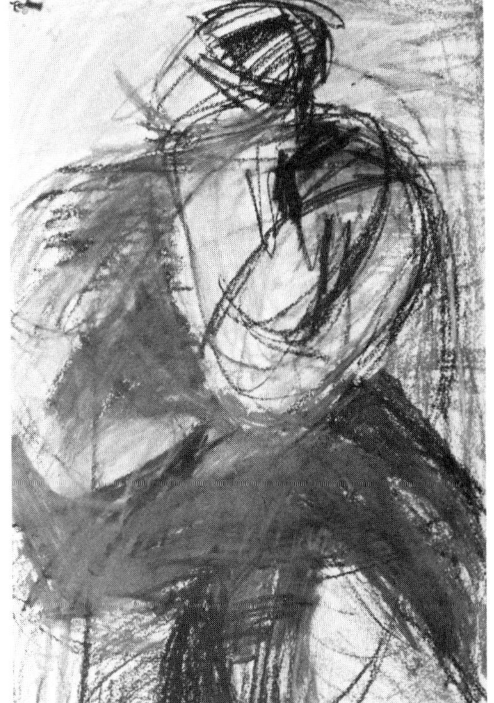

Figure 5-21. Formal considerations must lead the way. Drawing, by Nancy Hanley (art major). (Jean Mitchel).

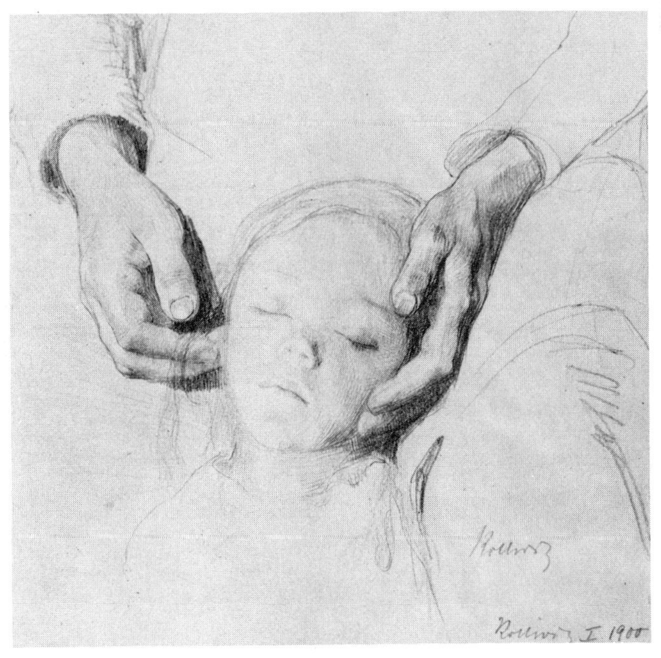

Figure 5-22. *Study of a child for "Downtrodden"*, by Käethe Kollwitz. 1900. Pencil, 8¼" × 8¼". (Kupferstich-Kabinett, Dresden).

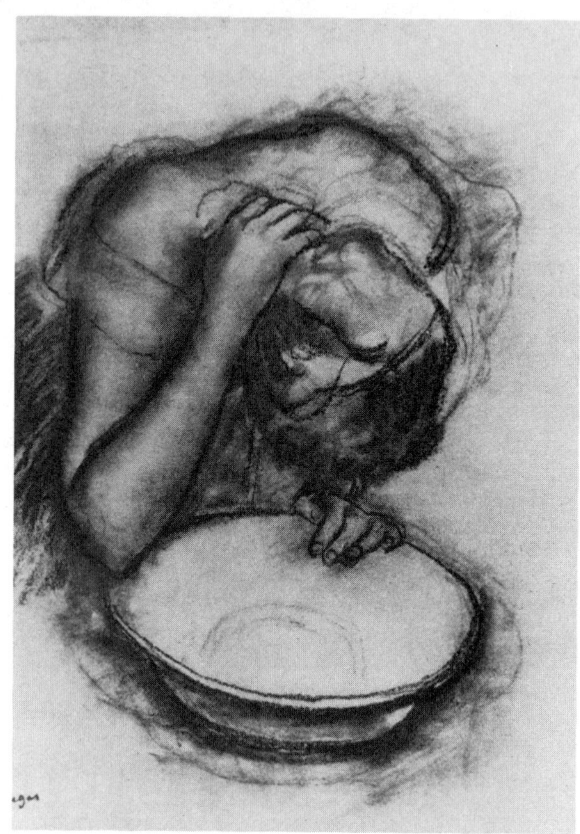

Figure 5-23. *Woman Washing,* by Edgar Degas. c. 1833. Charcoal and pastel, 24½″ × 18½″. Reprinted, with permission, from *Degas' Drawings* (Dover Publications, Inc., New York, 1973.

Figure 5-24. Crayon Drawing, by Balthus. 27½″ × 38⅜″. (Galerie Claude Bernard, Paris).

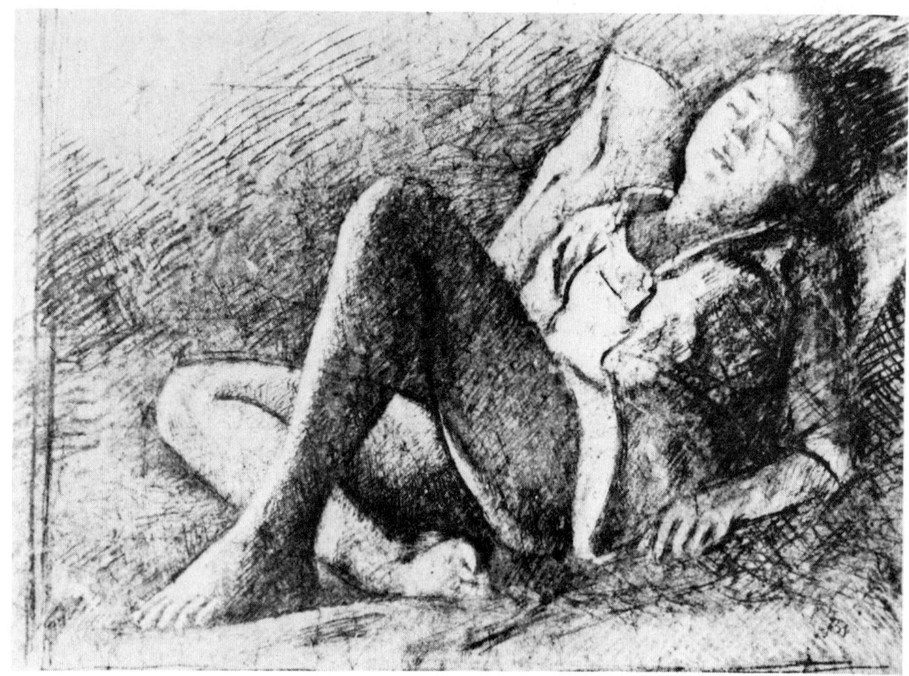

must be fed into the work to keep it alive. The explicit choices, nuances, and inferences that come together in the ultimate work are too intimately bound up in subjective experience, too dependent on spontaneous discovery, to translate into words.

We often complete a sustained study with the haunting knowledge that as our critical ability grows, we shall see that much should have been revised. Our hope is that something of interest will remain in the work for a long time. And it often does. I look back in amazement at some of my own early efforts, amazed that I still find something to be encouraged about, despite the sometimes hypercritical eye that years of teaching, looking, and working have given me.

The quick studies you try in conjunction with sustained work should include collage studies of the model, compositional studies of paintings and other two-dimensional objects, and perhaps black, white, and gray acrylic paint studies of a model. Collage, with its capacity for creating instant mass, is a perfect medium for drawing the room environment. Models' poses for collage studies shouldn't be any longer than fifteen to twenty minutes so you don't bog down in the technical aspects of the medium. Too much attention to detail—cutting too precisely, cementing better than is necessary, and the like—can cause you to lose track of the importance of *seeing* with the medium. Do three or four consecutive studies so that you don't have time to think about what they look like until all of them are done.

To do the collages you will need several corrugated cardboard rectangles of various sizes and shapes, a pair of utility scissors, rubber cement (be sure to have

ventilation), and some colored paper from magazines, wrapping paper, and so forth; avoid papers with "cute" textures. Let your work method create the texture. You can tear the paper as well as cut it, and the variety of edges created by tearing *and* cutting will serve you well. As suggested in the Chapter 4 description of collage studies of artwork, be free and rough with these studies. Try not to spend more than fifteen minutes with any one study. Let the studies stay loose and open.

The essential difference between these studies and the collage approach described in Chapter 4 is that collages from the model are your own compositions, while compositional studies attempt to understand ideas which already exist.

If you really want to challenge yourself, try quick studies done in black, white, and gray acrylic paint. For these works you need a tube of black and a tube of white acrylic paint, a piece of cardboard (or other primitive palette), two No. 8 bristle brushes, a jar of water for thinning the paint and keeping the brushes clean, and some paper towels. Instead of using paper, use several pieces of corrugated cardboard in various sizes ranging from 8 to 24 inches or more. Onto your makeshift palette squeeze out a generous amount of white, a generous amount of black, and also a black and white mixture to use as a middle gray. You should make every effort to stay with three values so that your work will be simple and clear. Start with a brush drawing in any value you wish, showing the general lines of the environment and the model. Then put down as quickly and broadly as you can the darks, the middle values, and the lights—in that order. Keep the

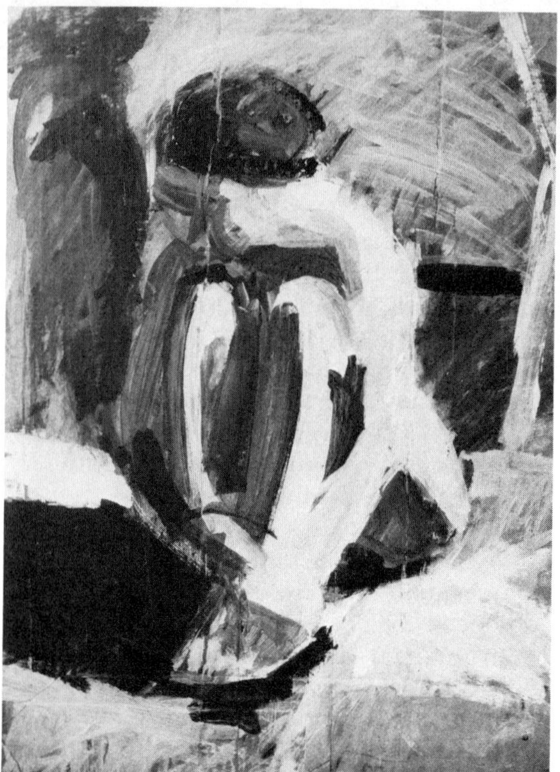

Figure 5-25. Keep the approach direct. Don't bother going back over your work. Black and white acrylic study, by Marilu Gruben (art education major). (Jean Mitchel).

approach direct; don't bother going back over your work. If you spend too long with these studies (longer than thirty minutes) you risk becoming too concerned with technique and the manipulation of paint, ultimately losing sight of your original purpose of seeing a value pattern and stating it as simply as possible.

SUMMARY

Lines as boundaries of shapes, and mass as three-dimensional shape can be dealt with separately or combined in counterpoint. Pencils and scissors are used for pure line. Conté, chamois, and kneaded eraser are the materials for mass studies and for line and mass combinations.

Mass has volume, air, and light; and moves in the negative volume of the page. In a mass study the subject is drawn in two values: light and dark. Brush and ink, dirty chamois, and clay are recommended as quick approaches to accompany the study of mass.

In sustained studies of mass and line both elements must be present from the first and carried through to the resolution of the work. Collage studies of a model and from compositions are appropriate accompanying quick studies. Studies in black and white acrylic paint are recommended for any user of this book who loves challenges.

Chapter 6
PLAY

They call me a "playboy," you know. I want to make things that are fun to look at, that have no propaganda value whatsoever.

Alexander Calder

THE IMPORTANCE OF PLAY

So far this book has dealt exclusively with structured exercises, on the premise that a newcomer to drawing needs a well-defined framework within which to grow. The purpose of this framework is to supply problems that gain a student's attention and direct his or her energy along productive and rewarding routes. But structure and problems alone cannot do everything that has to be done in the study of drawing. Structure has a way of ignoring the subjective side of experience, and problems do not always recognize the human need to relax and go one's own way. Too much structure fosters dependence. Play invites self-dependency, which is of crucial importance in any creative work. The ideal way to learn about drawing balances a structured, problem-solving approach with an approach that encourages self-direction. Such a balance works toward the development of the senses and the mind. A steady diet of play or a steady diet of structure would, either one, prove to be sadly insufficient in the context of a drawing class.

A problem, even one using explicit directions, should be designed so that the person solving it can reach beyond the

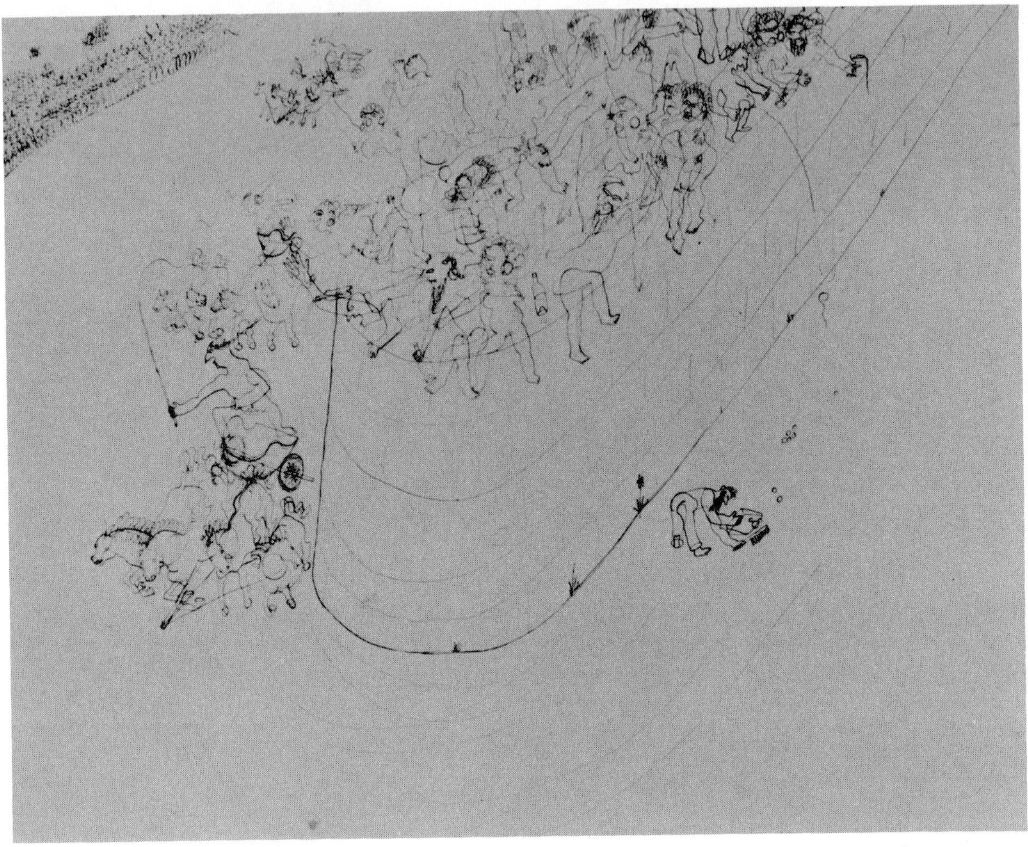

Figure 6-1. *Ben Hur* (detail), by Alexander Calder. 1931. Pen and ink, 22¾″ × 30¾″. Collection of Mr. and Mrs. Alvin S. Lane, New York. (Whitney Museum of American Art, New York).

stated goals of the problem. There should also always be carry-over into other areas of drawing.

DESCRIPTION OF PLAY

Play in drawing means willingness to use one's own resources, one's own voice, for better or worse. When you are really at play, you are content to let whatever happens, happen—no more dependency on other's values. Something in the spirit of play belongs to all creative work, not just to drawing or art. When you play you make your own work. The work can still be criticized, but the critic must use more universal terms than the restricted terms

used for work which stays within the guidelines of classroom problems.

To play means to let go, a difficult task for some people. Some of us have acquired an inhibited, false attitude toward what play really is. For instance, play for adults and young adults (the age seems to be steadily decreasing) means an organized social activity requiring goals as well as competition with other individuals or teams. Such play is, without doubt, helpful for staying in physical shape, developing teamwork, and preparing for the competitive world of business, but is such activity always play? If *to play* means to relax from a structured, disciplined routine for the sake of self-renewal, then the answer is no. Play, in art, is done for the pleasure of creating a dialogue with one's medium, one's self, and one's environment. The discoveries made in play would not be so easy to make in any other context.

APPROACH

In drawing, the ideal approach to play would be simply to sit down on the floor and start scribbling with any available material until you are totally absorbed in what is happening on the paper—until the scribbling finds direction. The only possible criterion for your choice of materials should be for you to use the material you find satisfying to work with.

If you find it easy to play in this manner, or if you have a teacher who can help you play so directly, then the only reason you should read the rest of this chapter is for the fun of it. But if you feel the need for a push into play, I offer the following suggestions as a means to prime the pump.

First of all, you must have a variety of materials on hand: pencils, a few colored pencils or crayons, ball point pens, colored paper, rubber cement, glue, scissors, conté, or any other material you may have accumulated. But before starting to draw, or even starting to think about drawing, take the time to make an observation trip. An observation trip is a foray, preferably on foot, into a neighborhood or down a street which you have reason to believe will be interesting to you. Or go to a store, like a supermarket, where you know people will be walking around, to a waiting room, or to a public event. A suburban residential street where all the people are either in their houses or getting in and out of automobiles may offer an interesting option. Of course, it is possible that *any place* is worthy of observing if you can spend enough time at it.

Wherever you go, try to take in everything you can about the place: people, trees, buildings, streets, sidewalks, light, space, and movement. Look for facial expressions, clothes styles, and hair styles. Watch the way people walk. Notice how they gesture to each other. Look for all the different ways of standing, sitting, and leaning. Notice the textures of walls, cars, leaves, grass, and of all the

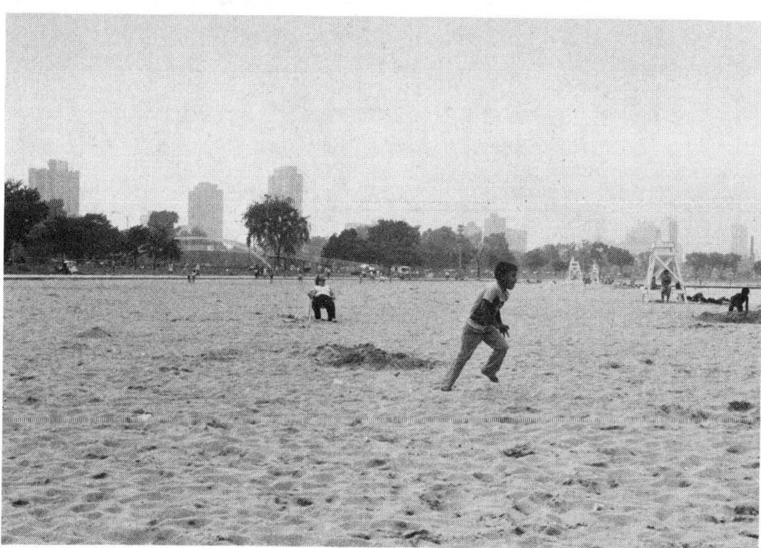

Figure 6-2. Wherever you walk, observe all that you can.

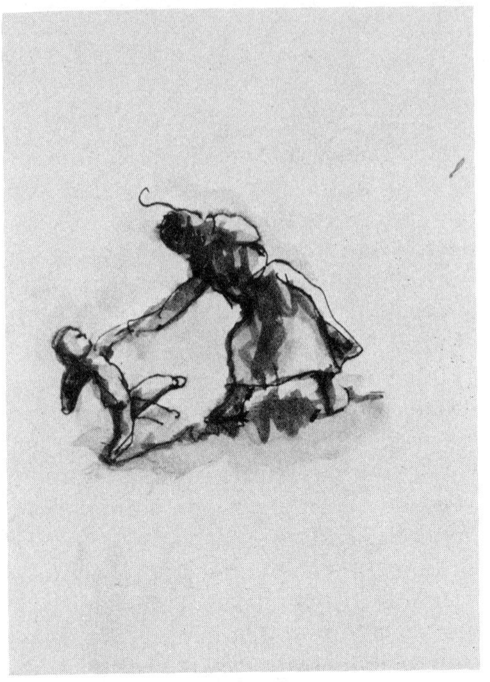

Figure 6-3. *Street Event—Woman Beating Child,* by Claes Oldenburg. 1958. Pen and watercolor. Reprinted, with permission, from Gene Baro, *Claes Oldenburg: Drawings and Prints* (Chelsea House, New York, 1969).

materials that you see. Try to remember patterns. Look for rises and slopes, or flatness, in the land. Note the direction of the streets and sidewalks; notice whether they are straight or curving. Watch the interacting movements of people, cars, clouds, and airplanes; observe the movement of paper and leaves blown by wind. Try to take in the mood, the *gesture*, of an entire scene. Is it sleepy? Humdrum? Troubled? What verbs are involved in the scene? Nouns? Adjectives?

Make a conscious effort to retain as much as possible of what you see. Ideally, you should go back to your workroom or classroom directly from your observation walk. Give yourself at least an hour with the array of materials mentioned earlier and start putting down anything you can remember in any helter-skelter fashion, without worrying about page composi-

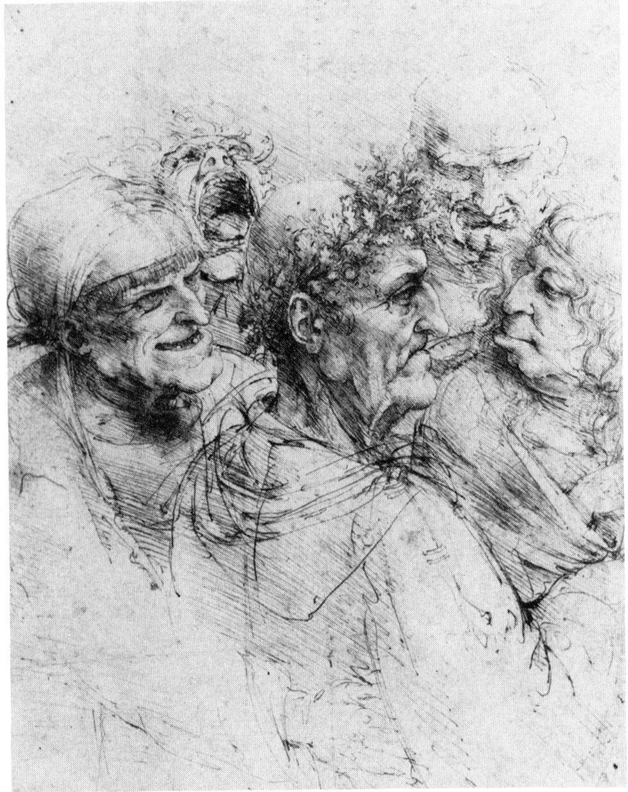

Figure 6-4. *A Group of Five Grotesque Heads,* by Leonardo da Vinci. 1490. Pen and ink on white paper, 10¼" × 8". Collection of Windsor Castle, reproduced by gracious permission of Her Majesty Queen Elizabeth II. (Curator of the Royal Library).

tion or a unified picture of any sort. At the start be very rough with your materials. If you are too careful, you will not only inhibit the method, you will also inhibit your memory and attitude. Your mood should be one of letting go, of letting things happen, of having fun. Don't even think about what your drawing looks like. Let it be ugly, or clumsy, or childlike, or illustrative. Fill up page after page with every movement, image, word, or phrase that you can recall from the trip. Relax and *let* the drawings happen rather than making them happen. See how strong you can be; how rough you can be. Break all the rules. Be silly. Be an iconoclast. Don't concern yourself about whether or not someone else has worked in the same way you are working. You don't need any outside authority to be yourself. *You* are doing *your* drawings in a way that only you can do them.

Make observation trips a habit. To vary the idea take a weekend trip, making notes on the spot as well as reconstruct-

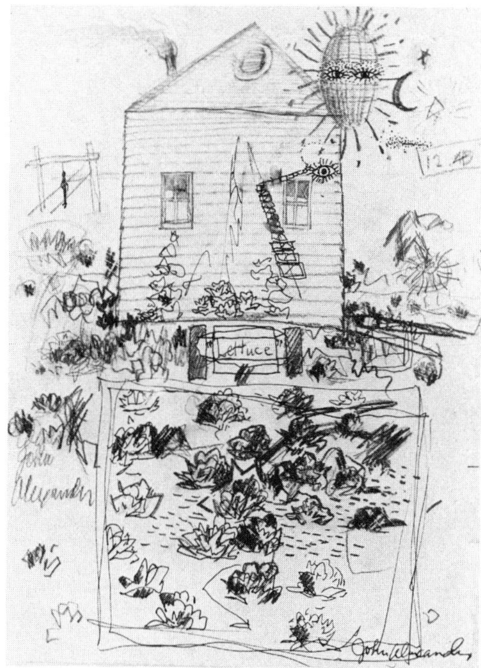

Figure 6-5. Instead of making your work happen allow it to happen in the spirit of play. *Lettuce Patch,* by John Alexander. 1980. Pencil and pen, 8½" × 11". Collection of the artist. (John Alexander).

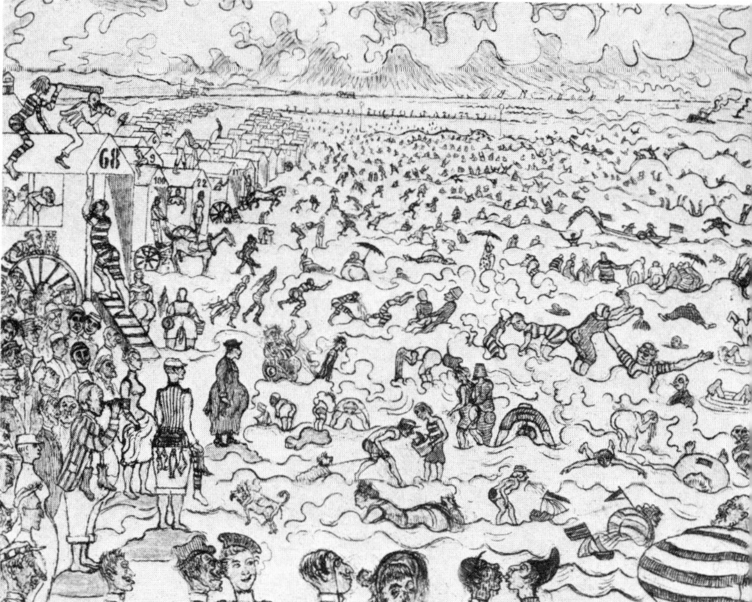

Figure 6-6. Break all the rules. Be silly. Be an iconoclast. *Beach at Ostende,* by James Ensor. 1889. Hand-colored etching, 8⅜" × 10⅜". (Art Institute of Chicago, gift from the estate of Curt Valentin).

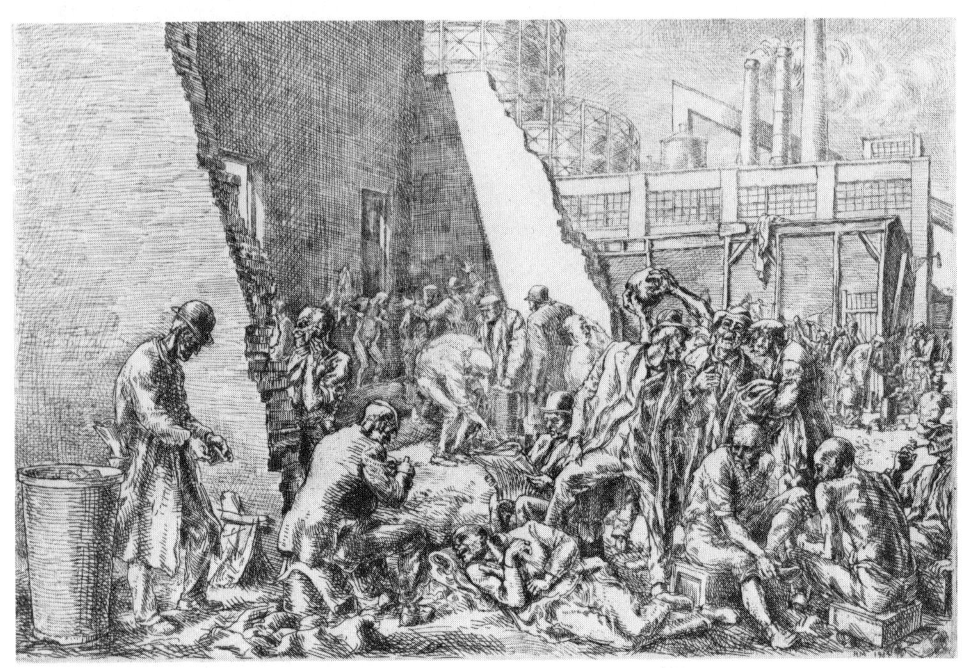

Figure 6-7. *Jungle,* by Reginald Marsh. 1934. Etching, 13¹⁄₁₆″ × 15¹³⁄₁₆″. (Whitney Museum of American Art, New York).

Figure 6-8. *Matches,* by James Surls. 1978. Ink on paper, 52″ × 72″. Collection of the artist. (Delahunty Gallery, Dallas).

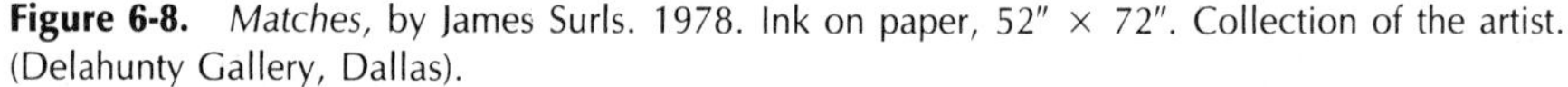

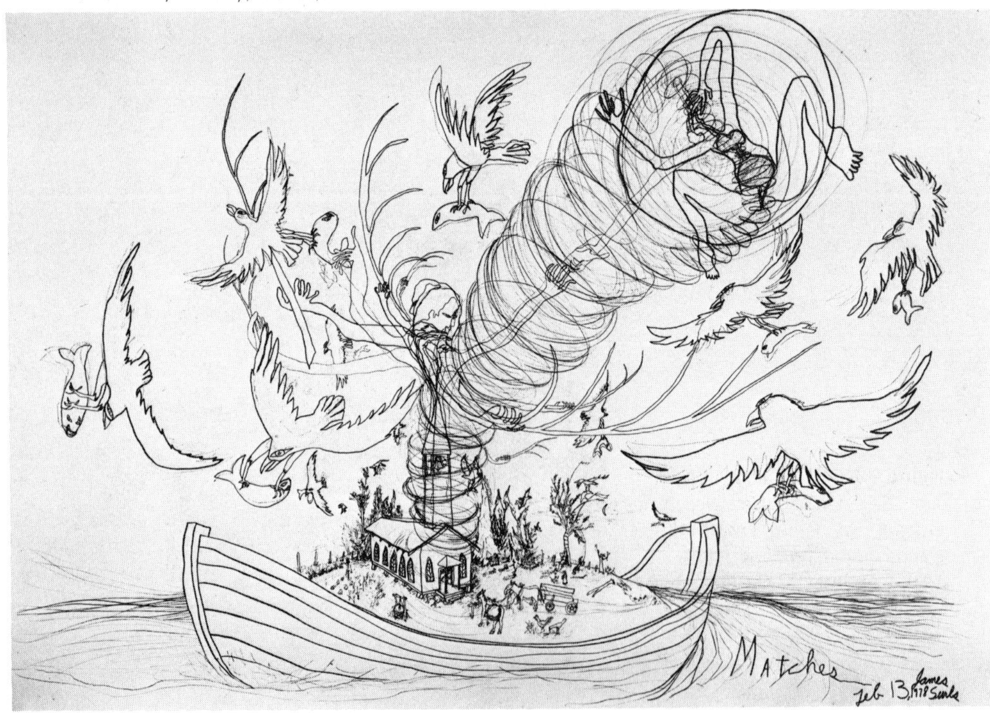

ing the scenes from memory after you return. Or take a bus ride (or some other form of public transportation) for the sole purpose of gathering material for drawing. The thing to remember is to do whatever you do in a spirit of play. Relax. *Don't rush things.* Playing takes mastery, and part of that mastery is learning to give all the time needed to the observation trips and the drawing sessions afterwards.

MONOGRAPHS OF ARTISTS AT PLAY

The element of play is present in all art, no matter how obscured by more predominant intentions it may be. However, playing is occasionally the obvious center of a particular artist's work. As illustration, I include the following brief monographs of four well-known contemporary artists for whom play is, or was, far more

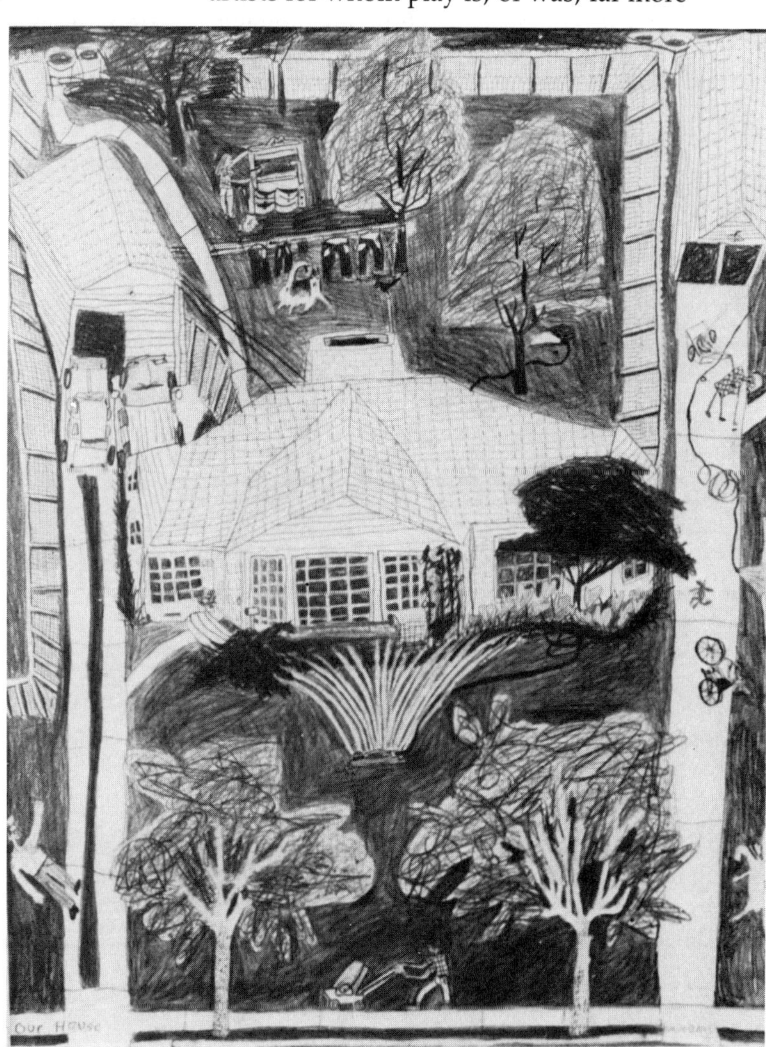

Figure 6-9. *Our House,* by David Bates. 1979. Pencil, 27¾" × 21¾". Collection of the artist. (author).

than a minor current in their bodies of work: Alexander Calder, Jean Dubuffet, Max Ernst, and Claes Oldenburg.

Alexander Calder

Alexander Calder was born in America in 1898, into a family of visual artists. Calder himself planned to be an engineer and earned a degree in mechanical engineering. But his equally strong interest in art led him to study at the Art Students League in New York, principally under John Sloan. Although an American, Calder lived off and on in Europe throughout his productive years. While his mobiles are his most widely popular works, the full body of his work is unusually extensive, including (in addition to a prodigious amount of drawing, painting, and sculpture) toy making, book illustration, and of course the miniature circus—an ongoing project throughout his adult life. Calder died in 1976.

Quotes by Alexander Calder:

We marvel at the tireless energy of the King of Beasts and his lioness pacing before the bars. How kingly and courageous they seem whenever we see them. Even in the circus where they supposedly are tamed, they seem ever to be on the verge of breaking loose.

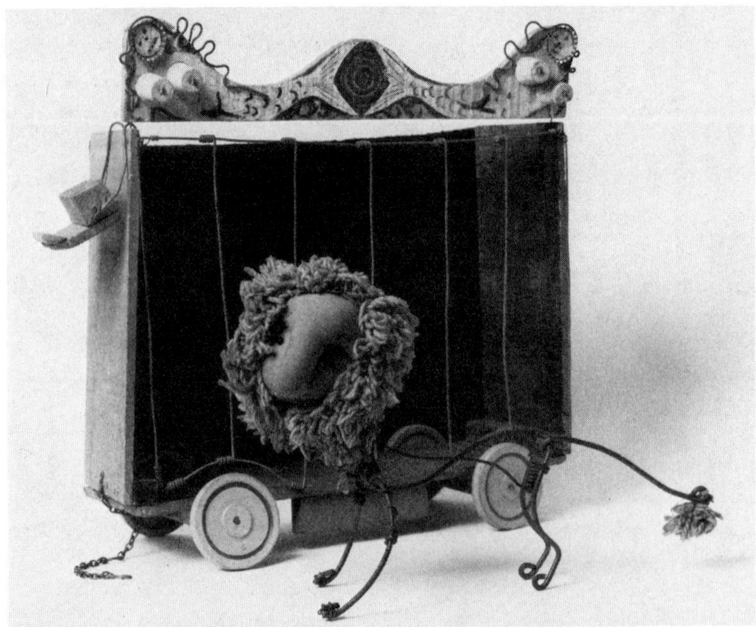

Figure 6-10. *Lion and Cage,* by Alexander Calder. 1926–31. *Lion:* Wire, yarn, cotton, felt, and plastic, 9½" × 16½" × 5". Cage: Painted wood, wire, velvet, cork, and metal, 17⅛" × 19½" × 17½". (Whitney Museum of American Art, New York).

I think I was respected by my playmates for what I could make out of wood and leather with my tools and hands. One time I even made an electric light plug out of a cork, a nail, and a piece of copper wire. But after drawing an enormous spark from this apparatus, I quit bothering with electricity.

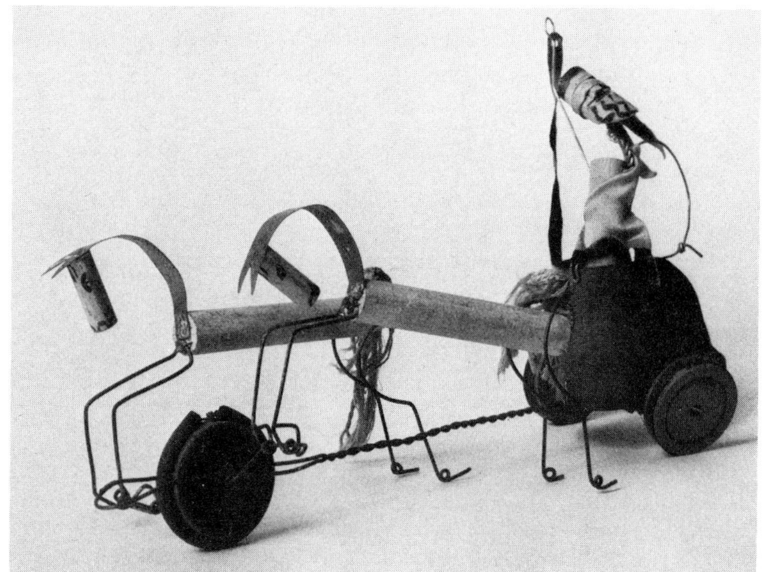

Figure 6-11. *Charioteer*, by Alexander Calder. 1926–31. Painted wood, metal, wire, leather, cloth, string, and rubber hose, 10¾″ × 19½″ × 8⅛″. (Whitney Museum of American Art, New York).

I seemed to have a knack of doing it with a single line.

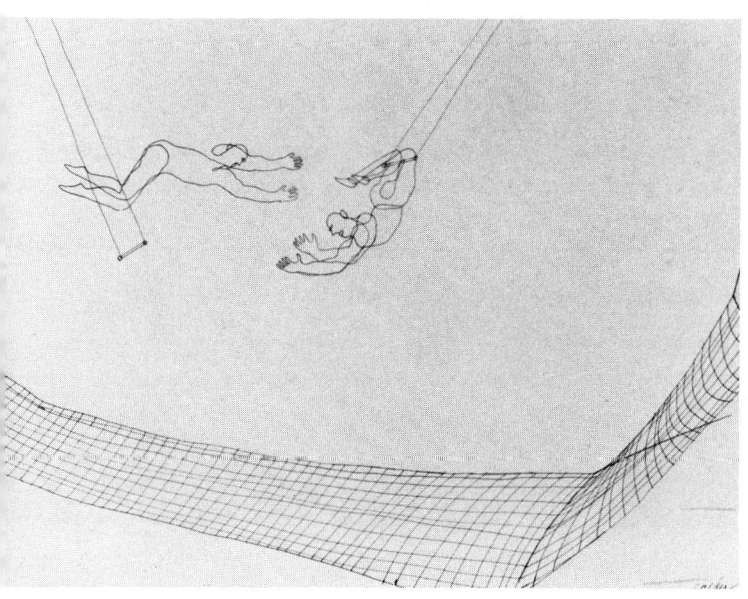

Figure 6-12. *The Catch*, by Alexander Calder. 1931. Pen and ink, 22¾″ × 30¾″. Collection of Dr. and Mrs. Arthur E. Kahn. (Whitney Museum of American Art, New York).

Jean Dubuffet

Jean Dubuffet was born in 1901 in Le Havre. He made several false starts in art, pursuing traditional Western styles, and only found his stride at age forty-five by letting his work follow his interests in naive art and "madness." His zealous belief in antioccidental ideas and disparaged values placed him at the front of the Art Brut movement. In the past thirty-five years Dubuffet has been monumentally prolific, producing many thousands of works in every conceivable medium from oil paint mixed with ashes to butterfly-wing collages. He is delighted by what he once called the "lively incompatibility" of materials which are not normally mixed, such as oil paint and water paint.

Figure 6-13. *Rue de L'Entourloupe,* by Jean Dubuffet. 1963. Oil, 35″ × 45¾″. (Galerie Beyeler, Switzerland).

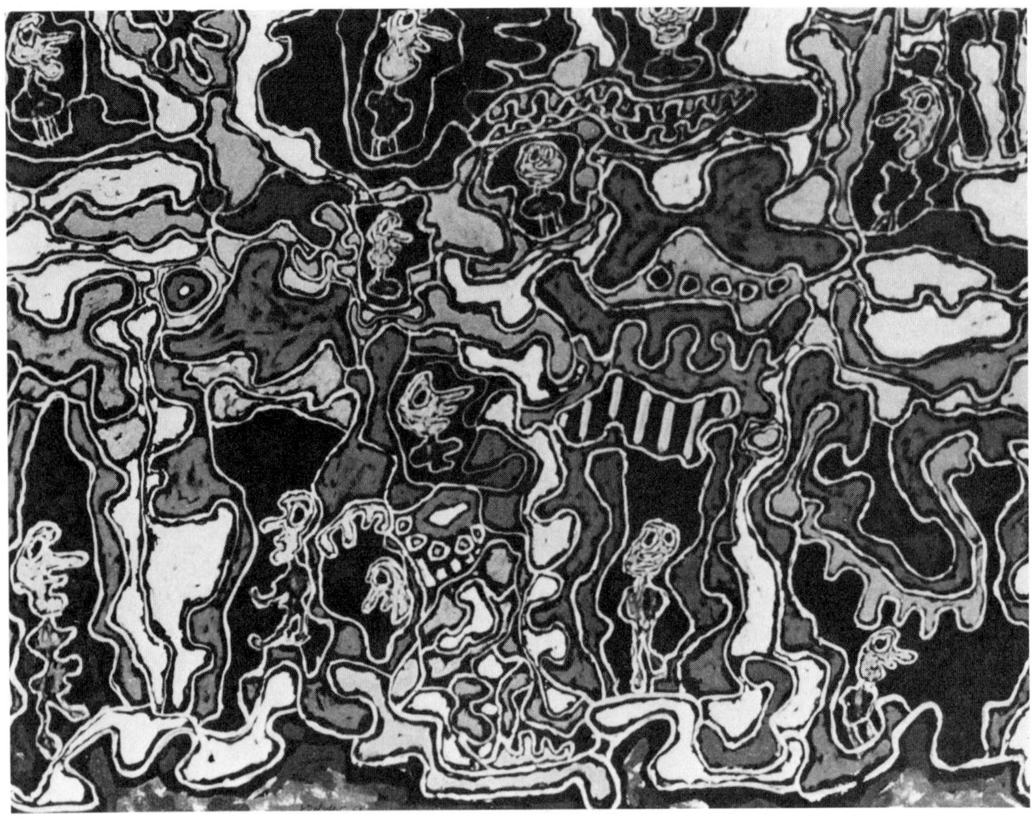

Quotes by Jean Dubuffet:

I feel a need that every work of art should in the highest degree lift one out of context, provoking a surprise and a shock. A painting does not work for me if it is not completely unexpected.

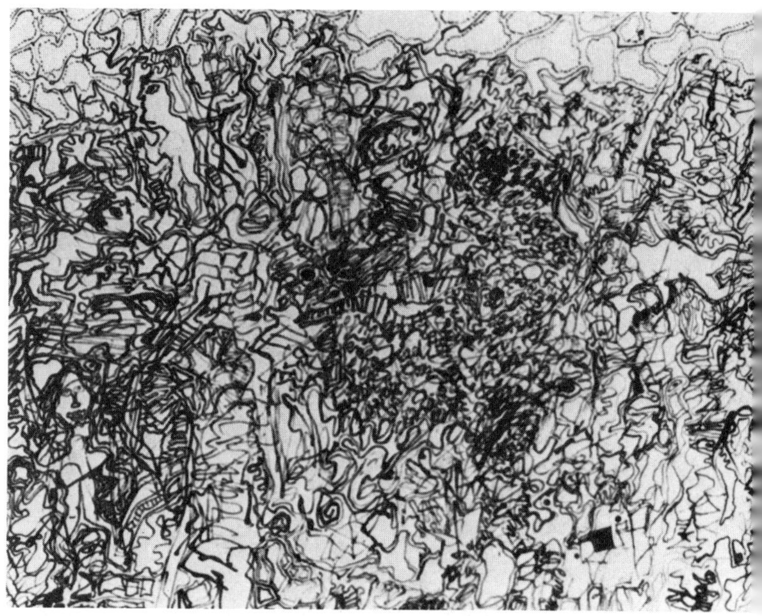

Figure 6-14. *Liaisons et Raisons,* by Jean Dubuffet. 1952. India ink, 20″ × 25⅝″. © ADAGP, Paris, 1983. (Museum of Modern Art, New York).

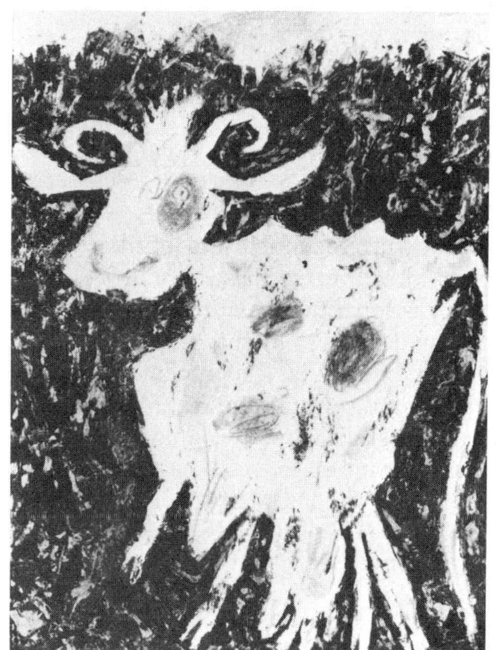

The idea that there are beautiful objects and ugly objects, people endowed with beauty and others who cannot claim it, has surely no other foundation than convention—old poppycock—and I declare that convention unhealthy. I enjoy, at any rate, dissociating, to begin with, this pretense of beauty from any object I undertake to paint, starting again from this naught. Very often this cleaning suffices for the object to emerge suddenly wonderful—as it is in fact, and as any object can be. The beauty of an object depends on how we look at it and not at all on its proper proportions.

Figure 6-15. *Vache la Belle Tétonnée,* by Jean Dubuffet. 1954. Oil, 51½″ × 38″. © ADAGP, Paris, 1983. (Museum of Modern Art, New York).

I think that too conscientious a scrutiny of an object distorts the normal mechanism of looking, and I believe that a painter should be very careful to keep himself from over-conscientiousness, should (a very difficult kind of gymnastics) stick to examining and representing things without ever doing violence to that distracted, confused state of mind, that kind of hazy consciousness perpetually in motion, which is man's normal condition when the things around him strike his attention. That is why I have an aversion to drawing any objects from life.

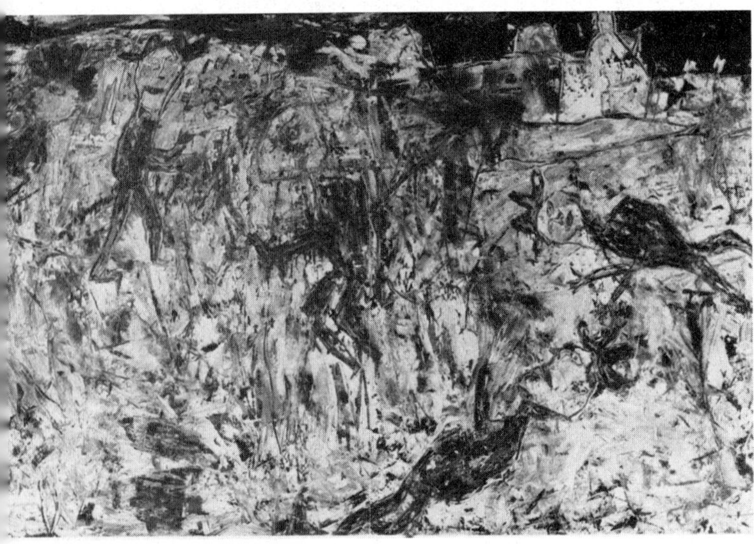

Figure 6-16. *La Vie Affairee,* by Jean Dubuffet. 1953. Oil 49½″ × 75½″. (Galerie Beyeler, Switzerland).

Max Ernst

Max Ernst was born in 1891 in Cologne, the second child of a teacher of the deaf and a painter. As a young man Ernst, along with other young artists and intellectuals of the time, revolted against the civilization responsible for the First World War, with its imbecilic destruction and its stupefying absurdity. Ernst's creative work in reaction to the horrors of war was not directed at society at large so much as it was a revelation of his personal emotional world, his dreams and fantasies. Through his experimental work in collage, sculpture, painting, film, and writing Ernst became recognized as a modern European master, his place in history a certainty at the time of his death in 1976.

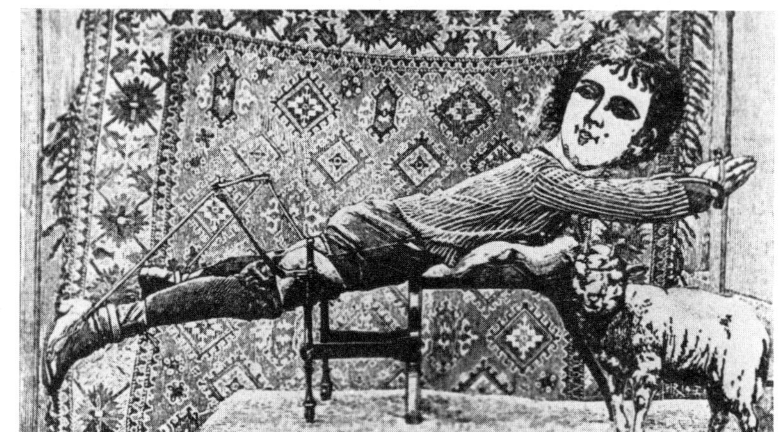

Figure 6-17. *Child*, by Max Ernst. 1920. Montage, 4⅜″ × 5¾″. Courtesy of Galeria Schwarz, Milan and Galerie Krugler, Geneva. (Attilio Bacci, Milan).

Quotes by Max Ernst:

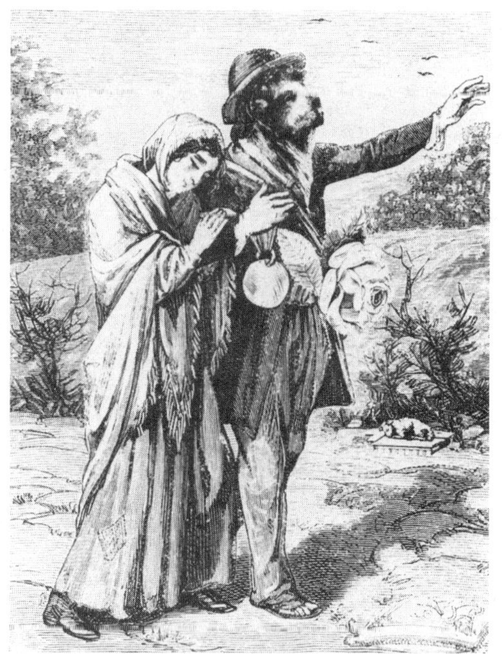

Collage technique is the systematic exploitation of the fortuitous or engineered encounter of two or more intrinsically incompatible realities on a surface which is manifestly inappropriate for the purpose— and the spark of poetry which leaps across the gap as these two realities are brought together.

Figure 6-18. From *Une Semaine de Bonté. A Surrealistic Novel in Collage,* by Max Ernst. 1934. © Estate of Max Ernst, 1982. (SPA-DEM, Paris/VAGA, New York).

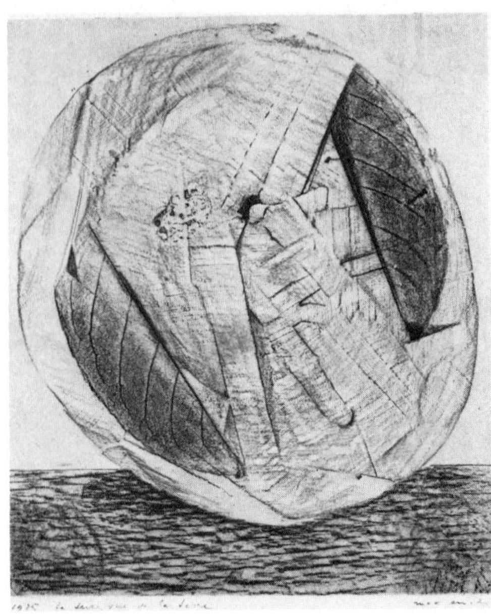

Figure 6-19. *The Earth Seen from the Earth*, by Max Ernst. 1925. Frottage. (Menil Foundation, Inc., Houston).

My wanderings, my unrest, my impatience, my doubts, my beliefs, my hallucinations, my loves, my outbursts of anger, my revolts, my contradictions, my refusals to submit to any discipline . . . have not created a climate favourable to the creation of a peaceful, serene work. My work is like my conduct: not harmonious in the sense of the classical composers, or even in the sense of the classical revolutionaries. Rebellious, heterogeneous, full of contradictions, it is unacceptable to the specialists—in art, in culture, in conduct, in logic, in morality. But it does have the ability to enchant my accomplices: the poets, the "paraphysicians and a few illiterates."

Tie an empty tin can to the end of a piece of string one or two yards long, drill a small hole in its bottom, fill the can with paint. Allow the can to swing to and fro on the end of the string over a canvas lying flat on the ground, guide the can by movements of the arms, the shoulders and the whole body. In this way amazing lines trickle onto the canvas. And then the game of free association can begin.

Figure 6-20. *Study for the Bewildered Planet*, by Max Ernst. 1942. 24¾″ × 25¼″. (Harry N. Abrams, Inc., New York).

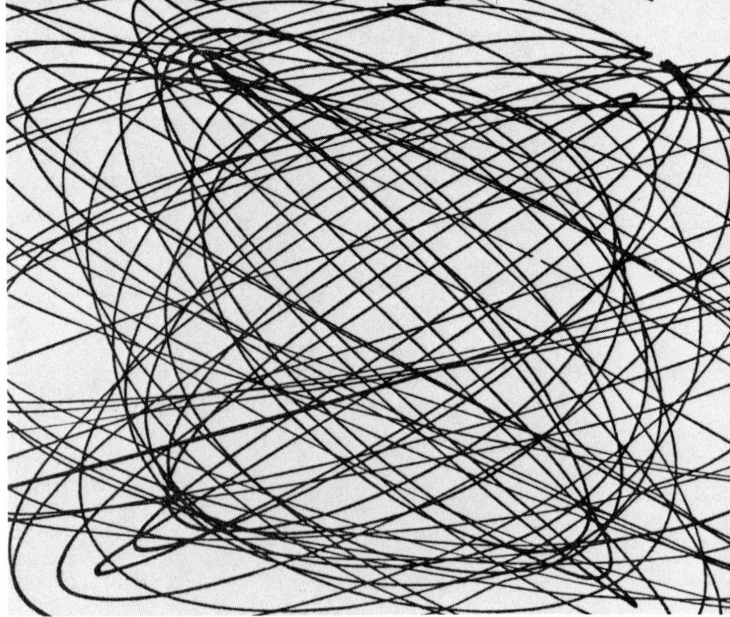

Claes Oldenburg

Claes Oldenburg was born in Stockholm in 1929 and moved to America as a child. He has been professionally active since moving to New York in 1956. His energetic production and breadth of ideas, crossing over pop art, conceptual art, primary sculpture, earthworks, and art brut have no parallel in contemporary art. His ability to draw is at the heart of his achievement.

Quotes by Claes Oldenburg:

Previous tenants in my studio in New Haven had scrawled over the entrance: "House of Mice." Throughout the studio there were signs: "Danger—Mice!" The studio proved to be full of mice who danced on the electrical cords as soon as the lights went out. When winter came, the rats returned from the fields nearby to gnaw on my sculptures of popcorn. A rodent subject was unavoidable.

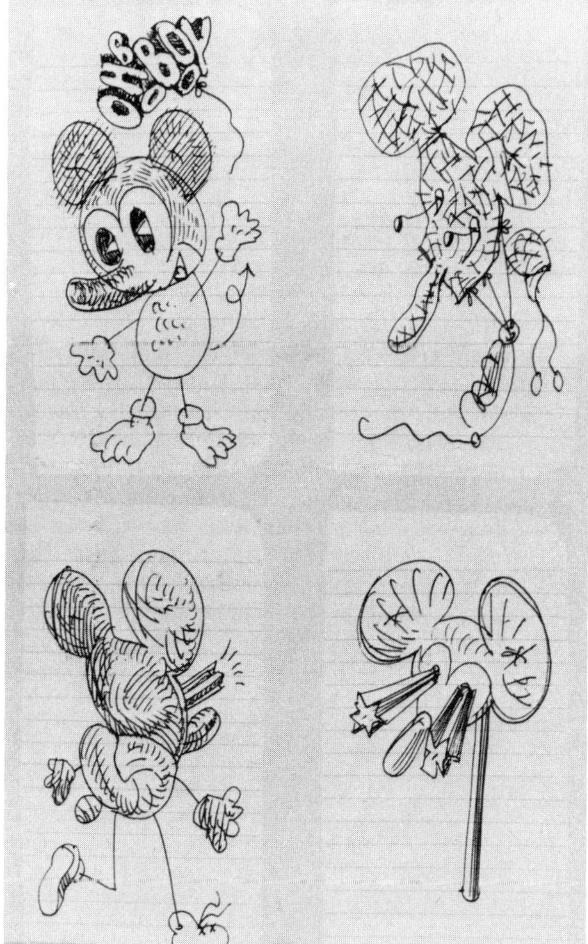

Figure 6-21. *Metaphoric studies of cartoon mice, OHBOBOOY, by* Claes Oldenburg. 1968. Ball point pen on four spiral notebook pages, each 5⅛" × 2¾". Reprinted, with permission, from Claes Oldenburg, *Notes in Hand* (Petersburg Press, Ltd., London, 1968).

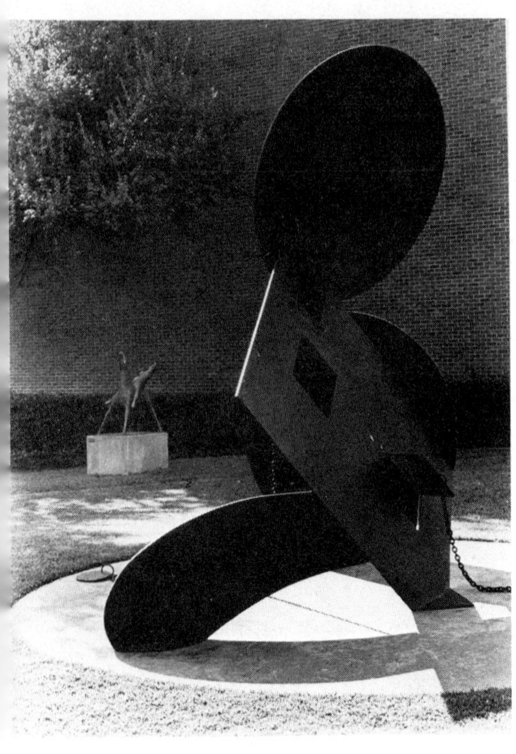

A field, perhaps a slope of Geometric Mice is envisaged to outlast us all—like the heads on Easter Island. Later visitors to this planet will wonder what purpose these figures served—if they were things or portraits or gods.

Figure 6-22. *Geometric Mouse II,* by Claes Oldenburg. 1969–70. Corten steel and aluminum, 144″ × 180″ × 84″. (Meadows Museum, Southern Methodist University, Dallas).

Some constructions use objects-in-action, or objects being acted on, like the Shattering Milk Bottle and the Thrown Can of Paint. The Shattering Milk Bottle was developed for a narrow site between two skyscrapers. The construction would consist of the whole bottle at several points in the air, the moment of impact, and the moments after impact—reconstructions of each incident simultaneously, like a strobe photo. Parts were to be attached to and imbedded in the walls, involving the entire space. The Thrown Can was proposed (but not executed) for the garden of the Museum of Modern Art. Paint hurled against the Museum wall—the act of hostility is transformed into a work of art, an example of the thing being attacked.

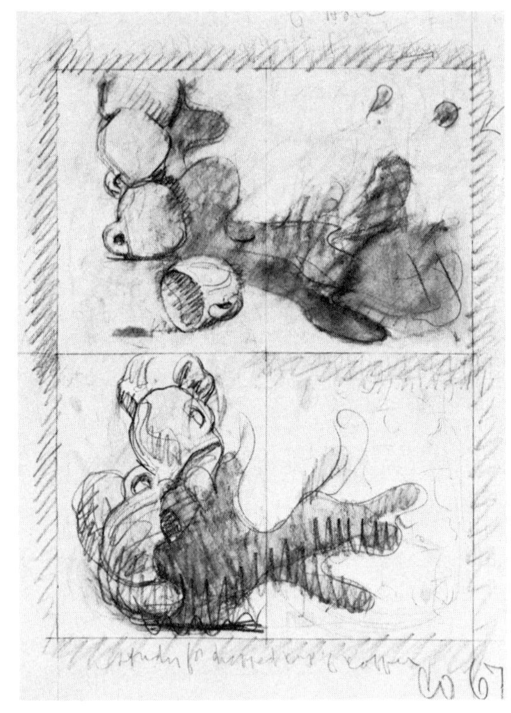

Figure 6-23. *Dropped Cup of Coffee—Study for "Image of the Buddha Preaching",* (by Frank O'Hara), by Claes Oldenburg. 1967. Pencil, crayon, and watercolor, 30½″ × 22¼″. (Museum of Modern Art, New York, gift of the artist).

The face is a cutout, like a mask, which is pasted on the diagram of the objects. The ice bag is also a cutout of different paper, pasted on. The face is divided in half vertically. One side shows the kindly aspect of the artist; the other, his brutal one. The body is introduced in the image of the face via the representation of the body's juices—the tongue (bringing out the insides)—which doubles as a heart and foot. The stare is partly the result of the working condition of making a self-portrait—one hangs up a mirror and stares into it—but also emphasizes the artist's reliance on the eyes. The 3½" on the forehead is left on as a reminder of my concern at the time with measurements of patterns. The Ice Bag on the head signifies that subject was on my mind. It doubles as a beret—attribute of the artist.

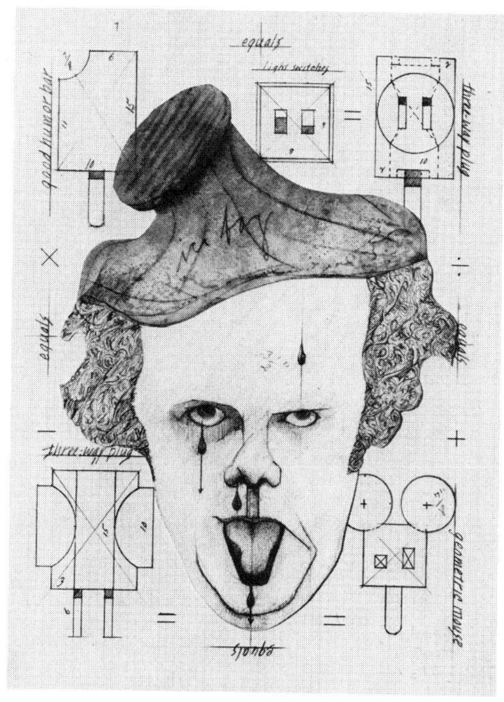

Figure 6-24. *Symbolic Self-portrait with Equals,* by Claes Oldenburg. 1969. Pencil, colored pencil, and spray enamel on graph and tracing paper, 11" × 8¼". Collection of Moderna Museet, Stockholm. (Nathan Rabin).

SUMMARY

All structure and no independent work would not be conducive to full development of the self. To play is to give yourself the freedom to do your own drawings. Criticism of such work requires a more universal standard than criticism of classroom drawing. To play means to let go—to overcome conditioned responses, preconceptions, and inhibitions.

Observation trips, followed by one or two hours of drawing with mixed media, are helpful to those who have trouble letting go.

Play is central to the work of some artists. A glimpse is given of the work and thought of four such artists: Alexander Calder, Jean Dubuffet, Max Ernst, and Claes Oldenburg.

Chapter 7
OUTSIDE SOURCES

Through a sense of connection with a system greater than himself man achieves aesthetic satisfaction, and the more nearly the universal system, the deeper the satisfaction.

Edmund Bacon

Socrates, the point is not to know oneself, but to forget.

Jean Dubuffet

MOVING AWAY FROM ART AND SELF

As important as self-discovery is to the student of drawing, self-indulgence—unwillingness to look outside oneself—leads to stagnation. Similarly, any approach to drawing which grows entirely out of existing ideas about drawing is destined to become an overrefined style: bound, safe, unable to respond to life's experiences or to intellectual search and discovery. Drawing that exists only to perpetuate known attitudes and ideals about drawing reflects a self-alienation, a fear of the world outside art and the art community. In contrast, some of the most compelling, provocative visual work is the result of artists' interests in human activities or other sources not typically associated with aesthetic bases. For instance, the sum total of Islamic religious art grew directly from mathematical concepts. Engineering and architecture are always practiced within the constraints of human needs as well as in harmony with the laws of physics. Daumier's concern with the social problems of his time directed the course of the body of his work. The same is true in the works of Goya, Hogarth, Rouault, Rivera, Kollwitz, Shahn, and so on to a list much too long to mention. The constructivist's basis for art is often math, chance, numbers—

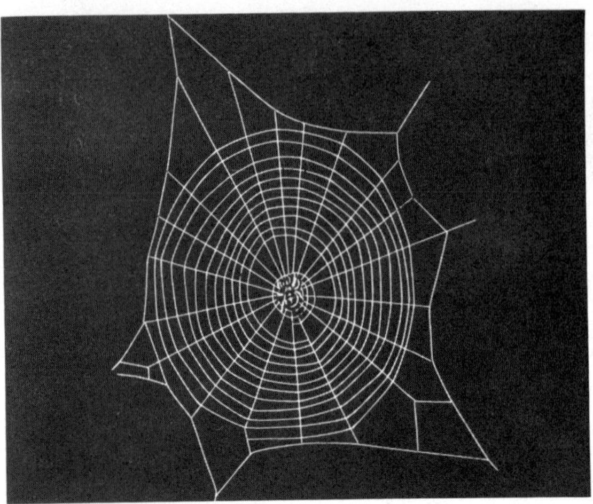

Figure 7-1. Some of the most compelling, provocative visual work is inspired by sources not typically associated with aesthetic bases. Reprinted, with permission, from Karl von Frisch and Otto von Frisch, *Animal Architecture* (Harcourt Brace Jovanovich, Inc., New York, 1974). (Turid Holldobler).

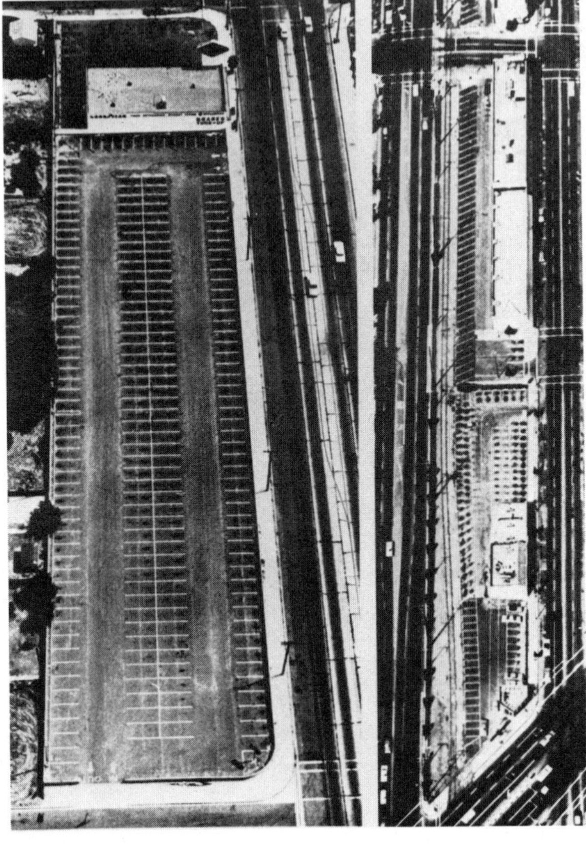

Figure 7-2. From *Thirty Four Parking Lots,* by Edward Ruscha. 1967. Reprinted, with permission, from Volker Kahmen, *Art History of Photography* (The Viking Press, Inc., New York, 1973). (Edward Ruscha).

Figure 7-3. Golden Gate Bridge: Engineering is always practiced within the constraints of human needs and in harmony with the law of physics.

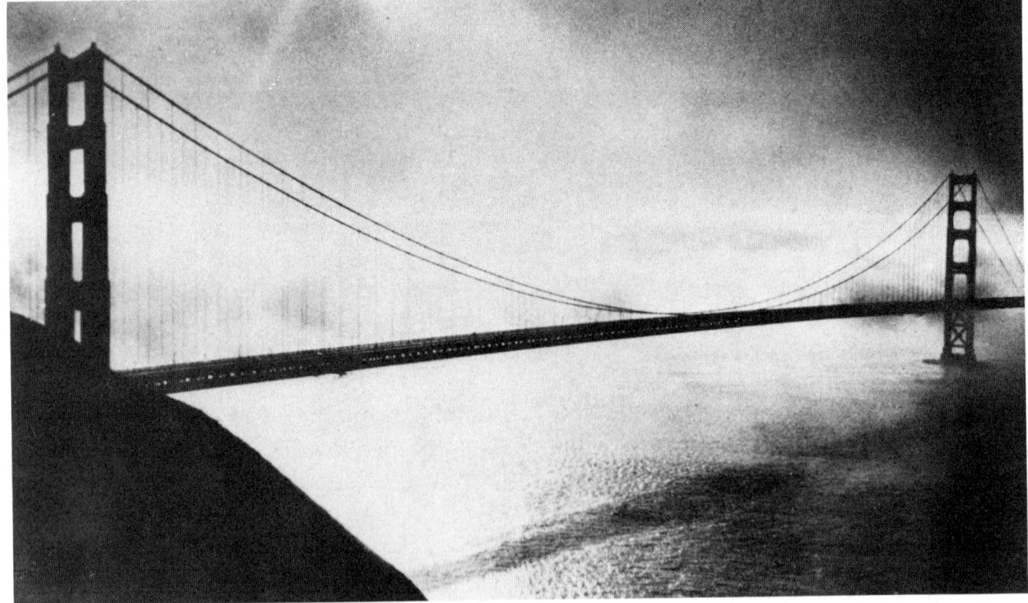

anything to help the artist overcome an ego-based aesthetic.*

As previously mentioned, Dubuffet's fascination with the thought patterns of children, psychotics, and the so-called primitive, became the motivating force for his mature art. Before his discovery (at age forty-five) of this source of motivation, he made several false starts in art, each of them suffocated by close ties to traditional Western aesthetics. Mark Tobey, also at age forty-five, found the universality he was searching for by a fusion of Eastern and Western religious ideas.

The power in these works comes from their creators' abilities to unite profound knowledge of art and self with a deeply-felt relationship to some larger, broader human experiences. Self-cen-

* "Constructivist" refers to Constructivism, the 20th–century art movement that championed a non–objective art based in general on geometry, hard edges, and an otherwise impersonal look emulating the perfection and order of objects built by machines.

tered themes and fashion seem to be an inevitable part of art, but those two concerns all alone can only have meaning within the art world. Alone, they further alienate art from the human community, reducing art to an insider's game.

My purpose in including this chapter is to try to show directions for reversing the inward path that art is inclined to take by focusing attention on worlds outside the subjective. I present the following projects as a few possibilities among infinite possibilities, as samples to be considered and to be enlarged upon, in hopes that they will help you look at the world with enlarged means and imagination.

EXPERIENCING THE ENVIRONMENT

Experiencing the environment is something that we do every day, sometimes consciously but more often subconsciously. In contrast, an urban designer is acutely aware of this experience,

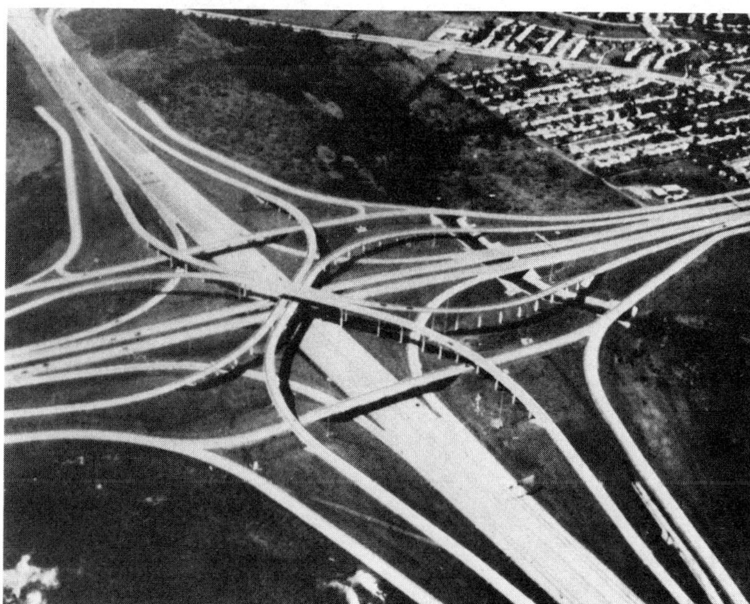

Figure 7-4. The designer articulates needs and controls changes. Reprinted, with permission, from Pratt, et. al., *Environmental Encounter* (Reverchon Press, Dallas, 1979).

whether the environment is natural or built, because it is the designer's job to articulate needs and control changes.

While an average person may see the environment in static passages, as if it were a series of snapshots, the professional designer has an overall, kinetic view, as if it were a movie.

The following words by Paul Klee exemplify a kinetic experience of the environment:

> *A man of antiquity sailing a boat, quite content and enjoying the ingenious comfort of the contrivance. The ancients represent the scene accordingly. And now: What a modern man experiences as he walks across the deck of a steamer: 1. his own movement 2. the movement of the ship which may be in the opposite direction 3. the direction and velocity of the current 4. the rotation of the earth 5. its orbit 6. the orbits of the moons and planets around it. Result: an interplay of movements in the universe, at their center the "I" on the ship.*

How could a drawing show the interplay of movements that Klee describes? Could it be done?

The following project will help you answer these questions through personal experience. The project focuses on the movement of mass in space.

To do the project, you must first go and stand for several minutes or more at a bridge with crosscurrents of traffic underneath, an escalator with a second escalator in view, a busy intersection with a traffic light, a natural environment, a shopping mall or other place where there is heavy pedestrian traffic, or an airport. As you stand at the place you have selected, record the movement around you with your whole muscular system, not just with your eyes. Think of the movements (as in the quote from Klee) that are invisible to you. Your questions to yourself might be along the lines of the following: What is the difference between the way an automobile moves and the way a person moves? Between the movement of clouds and the movement of a

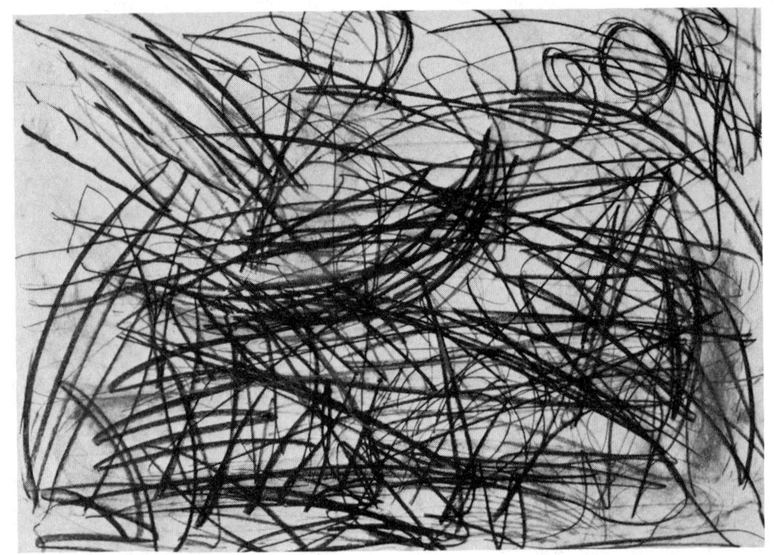

Figure 7-5. Mass in motion study, by Diane Dickson (art major). (author).

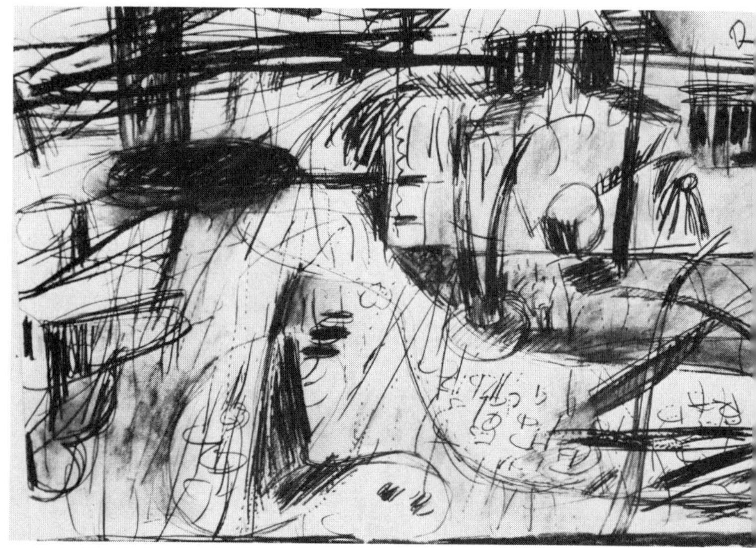

Figure 7-6. Look for the interplay of masses as they move in space. Mass in motion study, by Chong Chu (art major). (author).

tree in the wind? Is an airplane's movement the same as a car's? Which masses in the environment, if any, are still? Record in your body's memory the physical path of the various masses in motion around you. Which motions are linear? Which are vibrating? Amorphous? Spinning?

Now, start to think of all this experience in terms of a drawing. What will the components of your work be? Which medium or combination of materials is suggested by the idea? What scale do you want your drawing to be? Will you need to make a series of drawings?

Try to forget about the specifics of your experience. Movement and mass are broad, underlying ideas. Too much concern with details will only distract you from your original purpose: to study the interplay of masses as they move in space.

Figures 7-7 and 7-8 show works by well-known artists who were intensely interested in the movement of mass in space. Their concerns reflect long-range inquiry rather than brief interests. Each artist reached maturity in the 20th century. What were the forces in this epoch that led the artists to their positions?

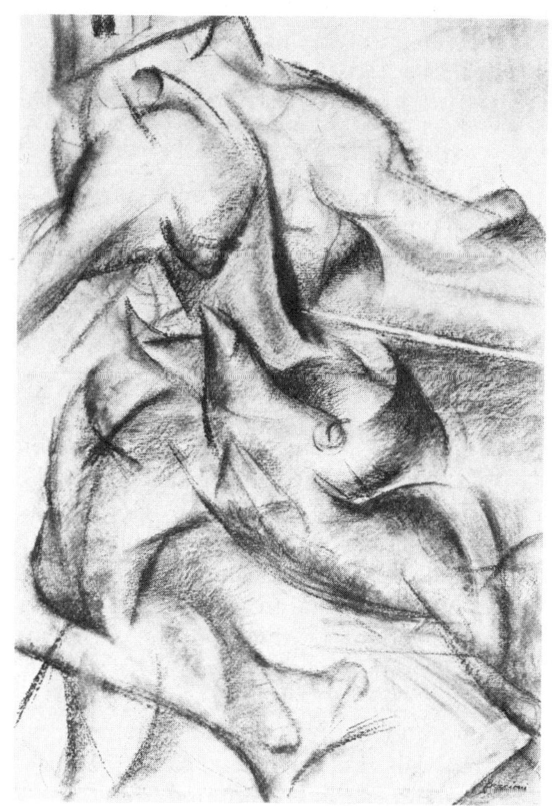

Figure 7-7. *Muscular Dynamism*, by Umberto Boccioni. 1913. Chalk and charcoal, 34″ × 23¼″. (Museum of Modern Art, New York).

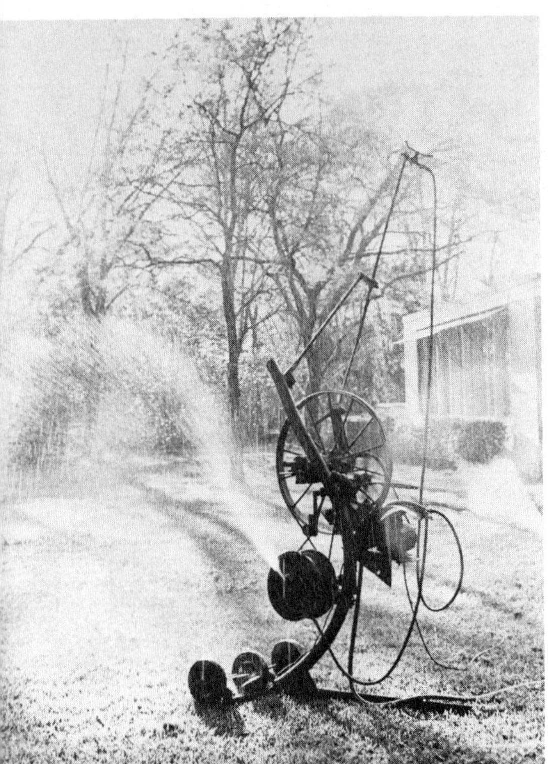

Figure 7-8. Fountain Sculpture, by Jean Tinguely. 1969. Scrap junk metal and motors from Houston junkyards, 107″ × 37½″ × 66″. Private collection. (Janet Woodard).

Have you seen works by other artists that show interest in the movement of mass in space?

SKETCHBOOK OF ANIMAL BUILDING

Building is an unconscious manifestation of the force of life. The body itself builds, in a sense, throughout life, by growing and maintaining protective coverings of various sorts. Most animals are programmed by nature to build structures independent of their bodies, either as shelters for themselves or for their young, or as traps. Techniques and materials vary from the plaiting and weaving of the materials that birds use, to the sophisticated line structures formed from the spi-

der's self-produced silk. Animals make paper, dig pits, and create mounds, tunnels, dams, and nests. Their tools are almost certain to be parts of their own bodies: the beak, teeth, claws, legs, and other parts—sometimes highly specialized—such as the spider's silk-producing mechanism. Animal building is often carried out with an economy that is enviable. Bees structure their combs with a repetition of the hexagonal shape, which has the smallest circumference of any of the

Figure 7-9. Detail of a weaverbird's nest: Many animals are programmed by nature to build structures independent of their bodies. Reprinted, with permission, from Karl von Frisch and Otto von Frisch, *Animal Architecture* (Harcourt Brace Jovanovich, Inc., New York, 1974). (Turid Holldobler).

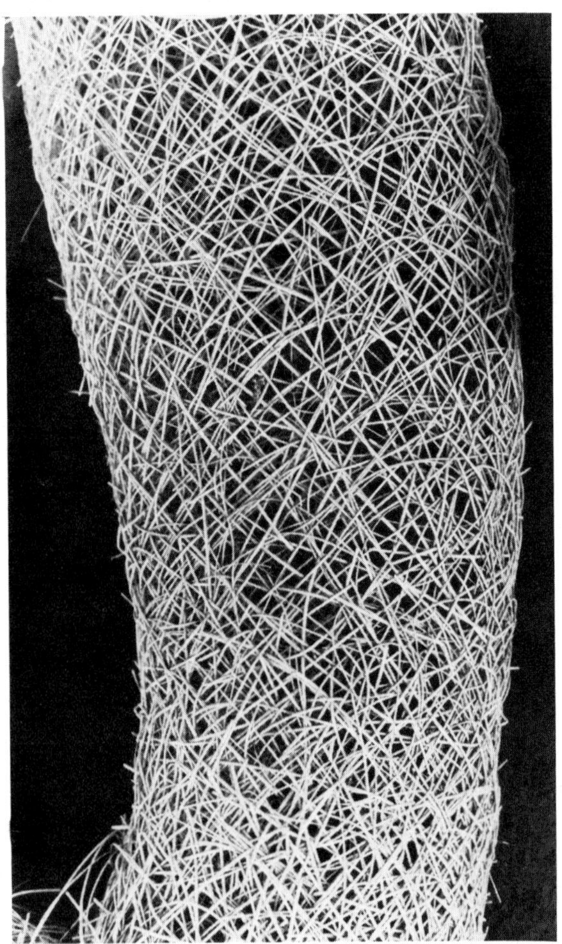

other geometric figures, and therefore requires the least amount of building material. Also, the comb, like the geometry of Islamic mosques, is a lesson in the kind of space we live in and how it can be divided.

Finding examples of animal architecture, either in reality (which is more exciting) or in photographic form, can be a stimulating source for a sketchbook exercise. There is great variety to be found, from the ant lion's pit to exquisitely woven bird's nests and the shells of sea animals. Sometimes we are able to make

provocative comparisons to human building, as in the beaver's dam.

As a sketchbook project, using any materials on hand, keep a drawn and verbal record of every form of animal building you can find during a given period of time, perhaps a few weeks. When the time is up, look through your work and see if you can find any underlying design similarities or principles (pattern, shape, line, texture, or idea). It may be the similarity between the ovoid form of a potter wasp's nest and the nest of a weaver bird, or perhaps you will note a hexagonal or

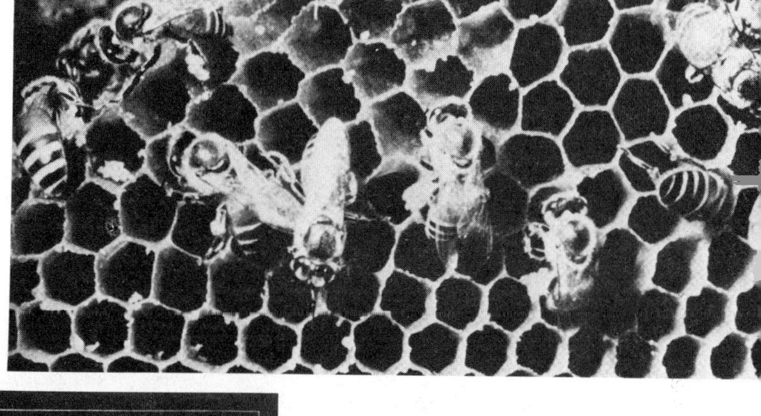

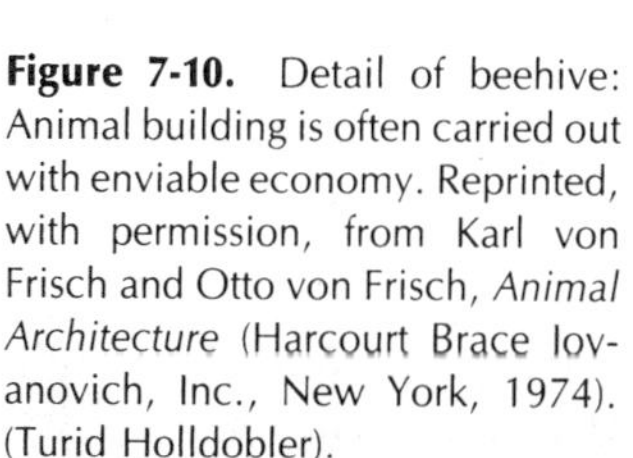

Figure 7-10. Detail of beehive: Animal building is often carried out with enviable economy. Reprinted, with permission, from Karl von Frisch and Otto von Frisch, *Animal Architecture* (Harcourt Brace Iovanovich, Inc., New York, 1974). (Turid Holldobler).

Figure 7-11. Compare Stella's painting with Fig. 7-1. *New Madrid,* by Frank Stella. 1961. Alkyd on canvas, 6'5" × 6'5". Collection of Mr. and Mrs. Eugene M. Schwartz. (Burckhardt).

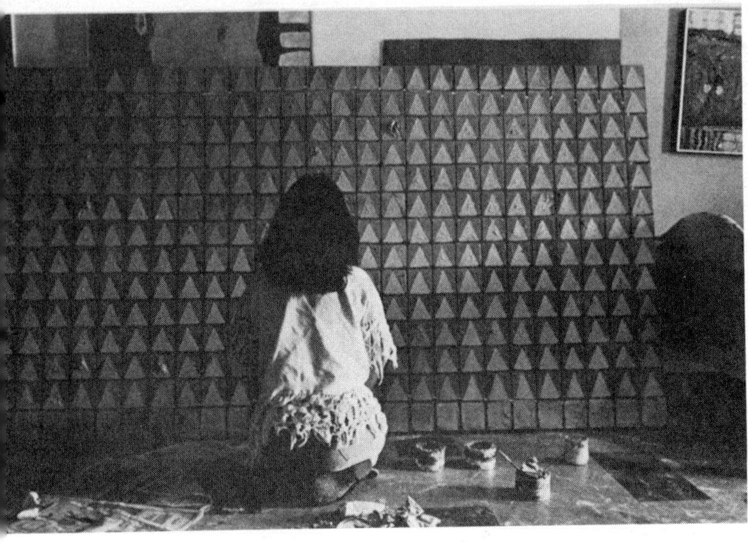

Figure 7-12. Jeanne Koch at work on a painting. From the catalogue for the *Texas Painting and Sculpture Exhibition,* 1976 (Dallas Museum of Fine Arts). (Lee Clockman).

spiral construction twice. Can you find any form of human architecture that relates to your drawing? Compare sketchbooks with your friends, perhaps in a class exhibit.

A MATHEMATICAL CONCEPT IN ISLAMIC ART

The mathematician and the Islamic artist were fused into one as a result of the Islamic commandment that forbade representation of images in religious contexts, such as mosques. For an alternative to representational art, the artists explored the mathematical intricacies of two-dimensional space. Such an exploration was presented and analyzed by Jacob Bronowski in his television series and book *The Ascent of Man:*

The Arabs were fond of designs in which the dark and the light units of the pattern are identical. And so . . . you can see that you could turn a dark leaf once through a right angle into a position of a neighbouring light leaf. Then, always rotating round the same point of junction, you can turn it into the next position, and (again round the same point of junction) you can turn it into the next, and finally back on itself. And the rotation spins the whole pattern correctly; every leaf in the pattern arrives at the position of another leaf, however far from the centre of rotation they lie.

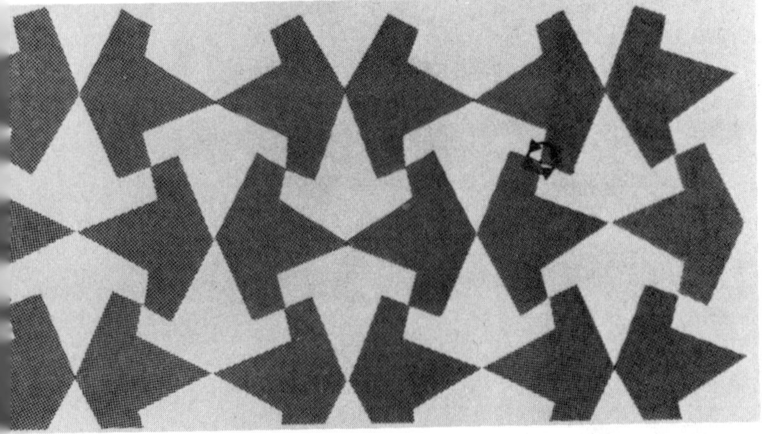

Figure 7-13. Diagram of Islamic pattern. Reprinted, with permission, from Jacob Bronowski, *The Ascent of Man* (Little, Brown & Company, Boston, 1973).

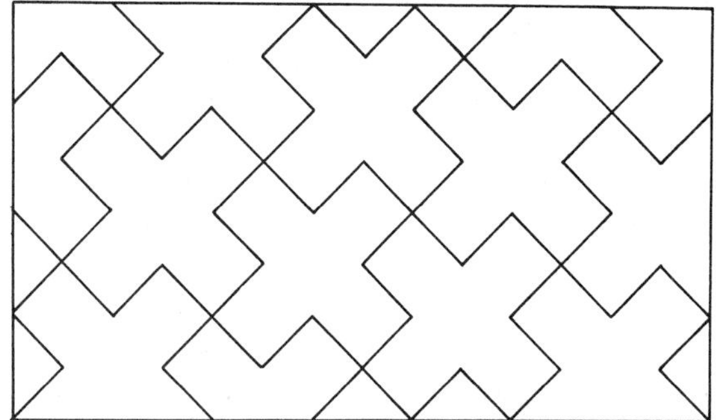

Figure 7-14. Diagram of rotating pattern: Carry out your motif in an overall pattern.

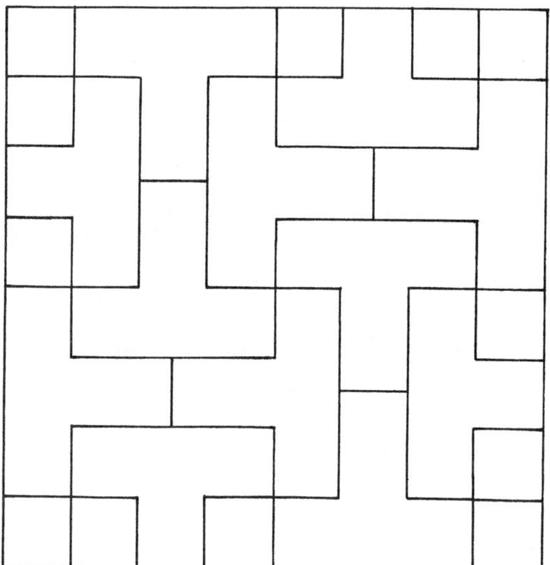

Figure 7-15. Diagram of rotating pattern.

In asking what laws will turn a pattern into itself, Bronowski, a mathematician, was "discovering the invisible laws that govern our space"—the special kind of space we live in, with its unbreakable properties.

As a drawing class project, design a rotating pattern in which each shape will move into the space of its neighboring identical shape, through at least two other identical shapes, and ultimately back into its own space. Use only two or three values in your drawing. Once you have found the motif you want to use, carry it out in an overall pattern. Use the material that seems most appropriate to you. Compare your results with the preceding sketchbook project and with the following project based on the laws of chance.

CHANCE

A few years ago I went to a solo exhibit of works by Gottfried Honegger, a prominent Swiss neo-constructivist. The form of each work in the exhibit had been determined by a game of numbers the artist had devised. Many of the works were made of thick mat board painted a bright yellow. I asked the artist why he had painted the works yellow, and his answer was an embarassed, "That's the Van Gogh left in me. I happen to like yellow." In other words, he had followed his sense choices, as Van Gogh would have done, by choosing a color he liked rather than by letting his game of numbers determine the color. He had tried to escape the conventional aesthetic position of letting the senses choose by basing his work purely on chance. In most respects he had succeeded, but using yellow because he liked it was, in his own mind, a flaw in the group of works.

Since Arp's exhibit of collages "arranged by the laws of chance" many other artists have experimented with similar ideas. Yves Klein left bare canvases outdoors to let nature paint a picture with mildew. Many of the photo-realist painters are willing to let the unthinking eye of the camera decide the facts of their paintings. Visual objects have been dictated by computers, preconceived grids, the toss of dice, or as in the Ellsworth Kelly painting *Seine* (Figs. 7-16 and 7-17), by pulling numbers out of a box. Kelly's dependence on natural phenomena (light reflected on water) should not be ignored, nor should his invention of a system of chance. The play of light reflections was reduced to a grid system and then filled in by progressing from the sides to the center, determining which squares to fill in entirely by chance. He pulled a number from a box, filled in the corresponding number on the left row of squares on the grid, returned the number to the box, pulled two numbers, filled in corresponding squares, returned, and so on until only one white square was left in a vertical row next to the center row. The same process was repeated from the right. By using this system he was able

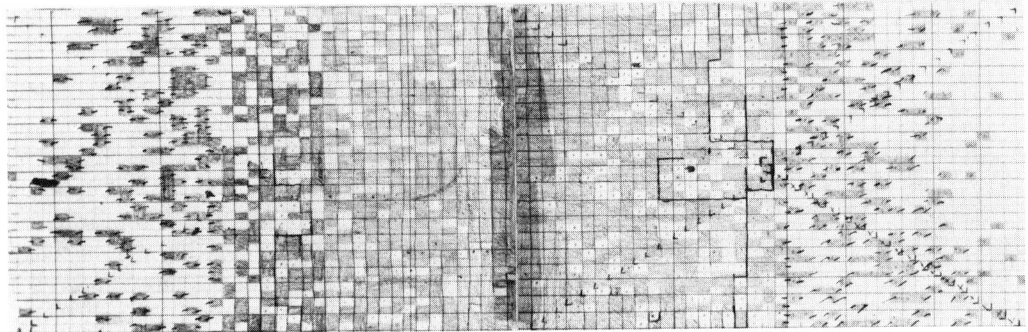

Figure 7-16. Chance diagram of light reflected on water. *Study for "Seine"*, by Ellsworth Kelly. 1951. Ink on pencil, 4¾" × 15⅞". Collection of the artist. (Eric Pollitzer).

Figure 7-17. The pattern was determined entirely by chance. *Seine,* by Ellsworth Kelly. 1951. Oil on wood, 16½" × 45¼". Collection of the artist. (Malcolm Varon).

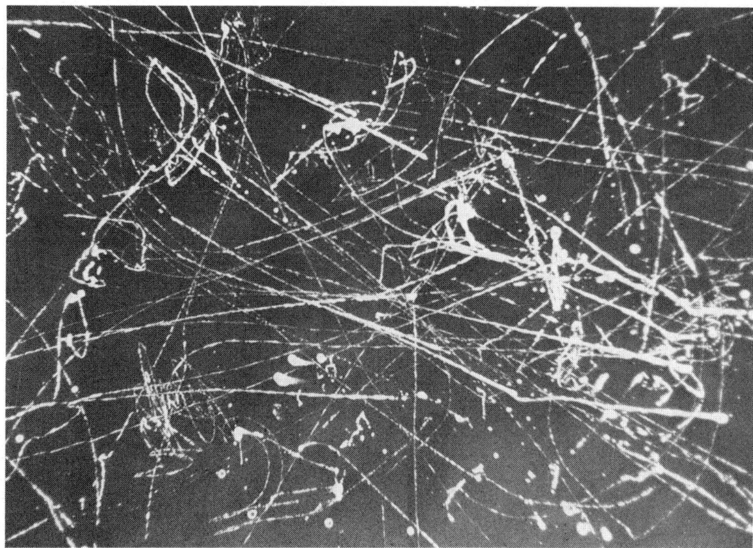

Figure 7-18. Marbles dipped in paint were allowed to roll around the paper. Study based on chance, by Cay Rose (undeclared major). (author).

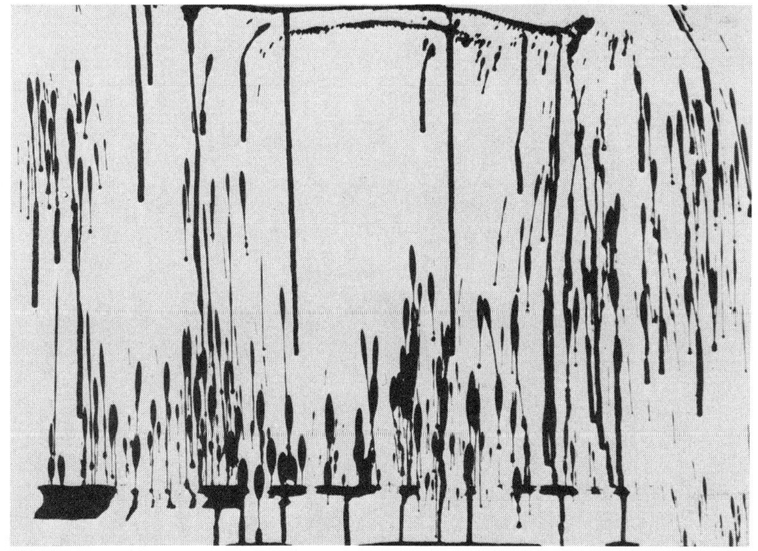

Figure 7-19. The lines were formed by allowing a fan to blow ink across the page. Study based on chance, by Matt Taylor (psychology major). (author).

to avoid a dependence on his own sense-level choice of which squares should be filled in and which should be left white.

As a project, devise a system to let chance create the form of a drawing. This is the only exercise in the book where you are asked to let forces outside yourself determine the destiny of your drawing. Your finished work should be compared with other works done in the class, and

discussed. Which works addressed the problem most honestly? What forces caused the individual differences in the works? What did you have to let go of in order to do this project? Did you like the project? Did it make you feel uncomfortable? Sometimes working in narrow limits causes an artist to think of many other ideas. Did you think of any follow-up ideas while working on this project?

SUMMARY

Any approach to drawing that chooses to stay unaware of forces outside of art runs the risk of stagnation. Many artists have built a body of work around interests in areas far removed from pure visual aesthetics: social consciousness, religion, mathematics, and chance, to name a few.

To direct work away from art and the self, projects are presented in environmental experience, animal building, a mathematical concept in Islamic art, and chance.

Chapter 8
CRITICISM

Quality . . . you know what it is, yet you don't know what it is. But that's self-contradictory. But some things are better than others, that is, they have more quality. But when you try to say what the quality is, apart from the things that have it, it all goes poof! There's nothing to talk about. But if you can't say what quality is, how do you know what it is, or how do you know that it even exists? If no one knows what it is, then for all practical purposes it really doesn't exist at all. But for all practical purposes it really does exist. What else are the grades based on? Why else would people pay fortunes for some things and throw others in the trash pile?

Robert M. Pirsig

ESTABLISHING DIALOGUE

Talking about art and listening to others talk about art is the first and most important step to take in the development of a critical sense. Most art schools provide built-in activities which encourage talking and listening: symposiums, colloquiums, seminars on art or related subjects, discussion sections of aesthetic classes, or—perhaps best of all—a local coffee shop or tavern where students, teachers, and area artists habitually congregate to talk about whatever is important to them. Each of us should try to take advantage of all situations which encourage dialogue.

Never let your fears keep you out of discussions, and when you enter in, take chances. Be candid, even when you don't feel certain about an idea. The best way for your doubts to be resolved is to get them out in the open. Your frankness and courage will help to generate a more spirited discussion than an inhibited, "leave it to the others" attitude. Just remember that the object of discussions, other than the sheer pleasure of dialogue, is to learn as much as you can about what you are looking at when you look at art. Through talking and listening you learn to articulate your thoughts, and you add to your knowledge and understanding.

If you can find no obvious source

for art discussions, start a student art group, or equivalent, as an arena for voicing ideas and listening to others talk about their ideas. An art group could also serve as a forum for inviting teachers or other informed guests to talk and lead discussions. Such a group must welcome a diversity of personalities and opinions. This is the best assurance against its turning into a social "in" group and losing track of its true reason for existing: Dialogue.

In addition to talking and listening, you must look at art. Art books, with their beautiful reproductions, make an hour's browsing in a book store the next best thing to a museum visit. If you can afford it, start a collection of books on art.

Keep a calendar of museum events. Go to gallery shows, and when you have the chance, go to artists' studios. Look. Look at everything. Don't be afraid to look at bad work: art fair paintings, over-the-couch seascapes, paintings on velvet, kitsch, and second- and third-hand avant garde. By becoming familiar with a great range of objects done in the name of art, you will clarify and strengthen your own ideas about what quality really is and isn't. Know when you like or dislike a work, regardless of consensus opinion. At the same time, listen to the opinions of others. Don't close your mind. Your chances of forming enlightened opinions are greatly improved by listening with an open mind to knowledgeable people. Don't listen to agree, but to weigh and assimilate.

Reading about art is an obvious method of developing a critical sense. Through reading, dialogue is established with a far larger sphere than a circle of intelligent friends. As with listening, don't read to agree; read to understand. If necessary, you must vigorously disagree. In Ben Shahn's famous book *The Shape of Content*, the author suggests that an art student read everything except the reviews! Shahn, like all of us, may have had painful experiences with reviews of his own work, and in that light, one can understand his advice. But I will disagree and suggest that you read the reviews as well. Of course, you should not read them to accept as gospel; they are never that. Read them for your own growth. None of us do ourselves justice when we hide from ideas that we fear. Isolation from painful ideas may bring a feeling of security, but it is the same security that one has in a prison.

CLASS CRITIQUES

The best way to discuss quality in your work and the work of your peers is through class critiques. A class critique calls for a sizeable pinning board where a group of drawings can be displayed for the entire class to see. Ideally, everyone present is involved in the critique; in other words, each person tries to express his or her thoughts in a most direct and candid way about any work or works under discussion. Students must also be prepared to hear others' opinions of their work, no matter how flattering or condemning the comments may be. Critiques often become personal events, not only because you are finding out which of your works are getting through to others, but also because you are saying what you think of other people's work. All is out in the open, up for review. Nothing is out of sight. Nothing is unmentionable.

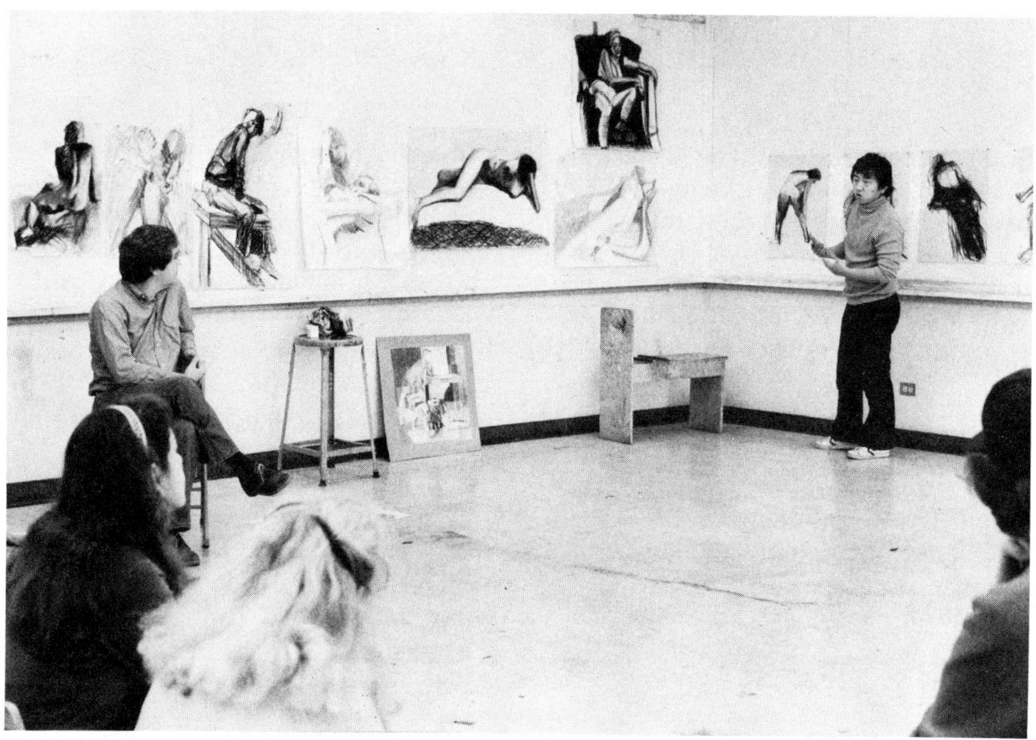

Figure 8-1. The best way to discuss quality in your work and the work of your peers is through class critiques. (Lynn Martin).

Only in this light can true criticism take place. When looking at pinned-up drawings, you can ask (or answer) some of the following questions: Do these drawings depend on gimmicks? Is technique emphasized over form? Are they honest works? Have the drawings been too influenced by a famous artist or by a member of the class? Who influenced them? Are there obvious problems concerning process? How can the process be improved? Do the drawings show energy? Laziness? Skill? Too much skill? What is the predominant mood of the drawings?

Invariably, a particular set of drawings will provoke particular questions. Don't depend on the questions listed above. These are only suggestions. Keep your mind alert. Tailor your comments and inquiries to fit the work in front of you.

GUEST CRITICS

A guest critic stretches the critical imagination by providing fresh input and by serving as a sounding board for your ideas. A class critique can be an exciting event if a guest is invited, even if the guest is no more glamourous than another teacher on the faculty of your school or an advanced student trying out new wings. *Never* pass up an opportunity to engage in dialogue with a visitor. Such an interchange will help you to see yourself in a different way. More than likely it will also affirm some of the most basic visual tenets that you have learned, such as the relevance of form or the importance of gesture. Even though you should show a guest proper courtesy (if for no other reason than you may want to invite him or her back), don't act like every word a guest utters is a heavenly law. If you want to defend a certain point, why not? You may be right. And besides, the idea of critiques and guests is for *you* to learn more about *drawing*, and you may be able to learn more through confrontation than you can by being quiet.

PAIRED WORKS FOR COMPARISON

The following group of works is presented in pairs, rather than individually. Through comparison, I can discuss the individual nature of each work more pointedly than it would be possible for me to do if I presented each work in isolation.

For a fresh view of your art, pair a photograph of one of your own works with a reproduction of a famous work in the same medium.

Grünewald drawing compared to a Rouault print

The Bible is the source for each of these works, and both artists were fervent Christians. While both works express the universal theme of suffering,

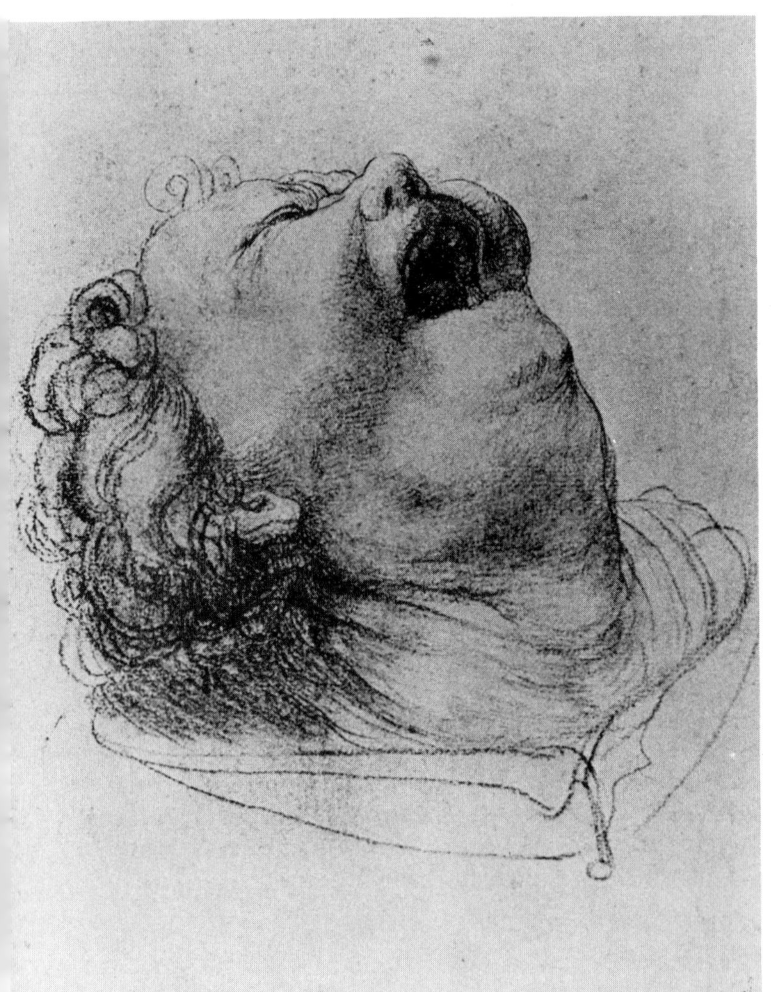

Figure 8-2. The feeling of air and light in the drawing betrays the artist's painterly sensibilities. *Crying Angel*, by Matthias Grunewald. c. 1515/16. Black chalk heightened with white by brush on light yellow brown paper, 9⅔" × 7⅞". (Kupferstich-Kabinett, Berlin).

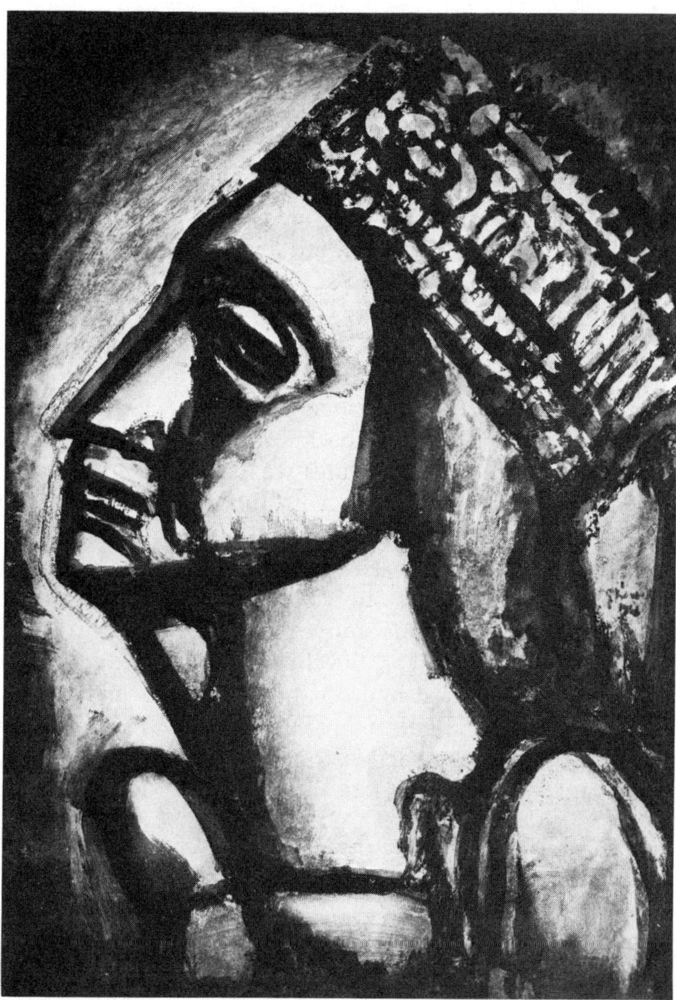

Figure 8-3. Rouault's direct means emotionalizes his work. *Virgin of the Seven Swords,* by Georges Rouault. Engraving, 23″ × 16⅛″. (National Gallery of Art, Washington, D.C.).

the suffering is related specifically to the passion of Christ. Matthias Grunewald's *Crying Angel* represents an open, unabated state of grief. Georges Rouault's *Virgin of the Seven Swords* shows suffering long endured and a willingness to accept any fate.

The two works are related by general content, but they are singularly disparate in approach. Grünewald lived in a time and place (Germany during the Northern Renaissance) where artists celebrated a newly acquired ability to make dazzling illusions of the everyday world but were still close to the late Gothic spiritual attitude; hence the religious fantasy of the drawing. And although Grünewald's drawing might impress us because of its three-dimensional view of the human head, it is not the illusionistic aspect of the drawing that gives it its enduring appeal. A lesser artist using the same degree of illusionism might make a maudlin and slick work. The quality of the drawing comes from its masterful synthesis of idea, illusion, and form. The dramatic scale of the head to the space of the page is softened, balanced out, by allowing some of the edges—the curls at the top of the forehead, for instance—to almost disappear into the light of the page. The delicacy (but certainty) of the transitions from value to value in the areas of face and hair also soften the impact of the large head with an open mouth. This feeling of air and light in the drawing betrays Grünewald's painterly sensibilities.

The line moving up through the right side of the face and around the forehead and first few curls of hair gives a superb shape to the upper background, which shows that Grünewald was as masterful with line as he was with tone. A rhythmic motif is established by repeating the double curved line of the open mouth in the curl showing above the forehead. The same movement is echoed in the hair, the ear, the cheek, the chin, and the gestural line on the right side of the collar. The drawing contrasts the gently curving line across the bottom of the page with the energetically curved contour line of the face.

It is safe to assume that this work was not drawn as consciously as my words make it sound. The quality of the drawing must be seen as spontaneously produced; as a synthesis of intuition and knowledge, discipline, and expression. And its quality should be seen as tied not only to Grünewald's talent but to his training and culture.

Obviously, Rouault's print is a product of a very different time and place in which illusionism had lost not only its challenge but also its magic. Naturalism no longer served the needs of artists living in a world which had become much smaller in a very short time because of improved communication. The significant painters of Rouault's time were leaving the objective world to photographers and moving toward subjective or nonobjective aesthetic positions. Rouault's

work evolved to an almost primitively direct means of emotionalizing the subjects and the structure of his art. The Miserere prints (which were first done as India Ink drawings) show his mature approach at its fullest.* Rouault, like Grünewald, reveals his painterly talents in the soft transitions of tones. But unlike Grünewald, Rouault reinforces his work with heavy brutal lines that evoke the leaded lines of stained glass. The features of the face and the anatomy of the neck and shoulders have been more than just simplified. They have been reduced to the most basic system of volumes. The system is then used as a structural building method manipulated to form the awesomely direct design that satisfied Rouault's expressive needs.

It is important to remember that Rouault's nonnaturalistic approach was a matter of choice rather than necessity, and that his mature expression passed through a naturalistic phase—it did not appear all of a sudden, fully matured.

Although it is not possible for anyone to say whether or not one of these two works will outlast the other, it is in order to declare that both artists were masters of their means; both works are strong in their individual ways; and both works are honest and learned. A work is inevitably a product of its time, but the strong work transcends its time and remains meaningful to future viewers because of its universality and levels of appeal. The Grünewald drawing has passed this ultimate test, while the Rouault has yet to be tested.

* A series of fifty-eight prints called *Miserere et Guerre* completed in 1927 and published in 1948.

A Philip Guston drawing compared to a Willem de Kooning drawing

These two drawings were done by artists of the same school (Abstract Expressionism), same country (America), and same time frame. The artists shared many of the same friends. And yet, we are aware right away that there are differences in the visual import of the two works. The Guston has a mood of intimacy and suggestion. The squiggles of lines are poised in the horizontal space

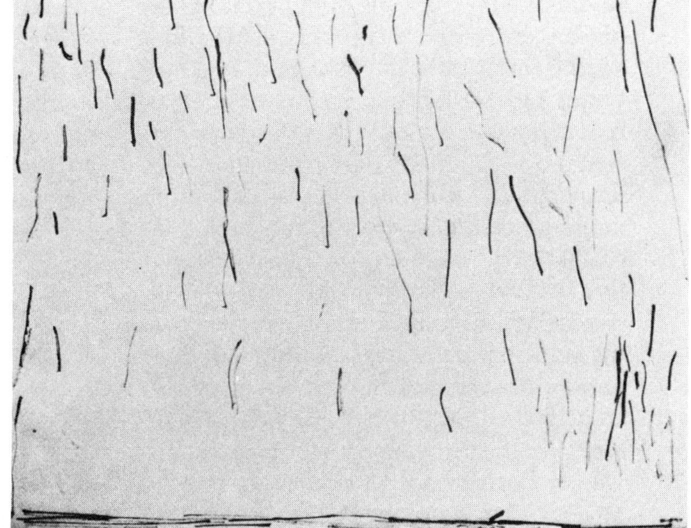

Figure 8-4. The lines are poised in horizontal space in measured relationships. Untitled drawing, by Philip Guston. 1951. Ink on paper, 17″ × 24½″. Collection of Morton Feldman. (University of Saint Thomas Art Department, Houston).

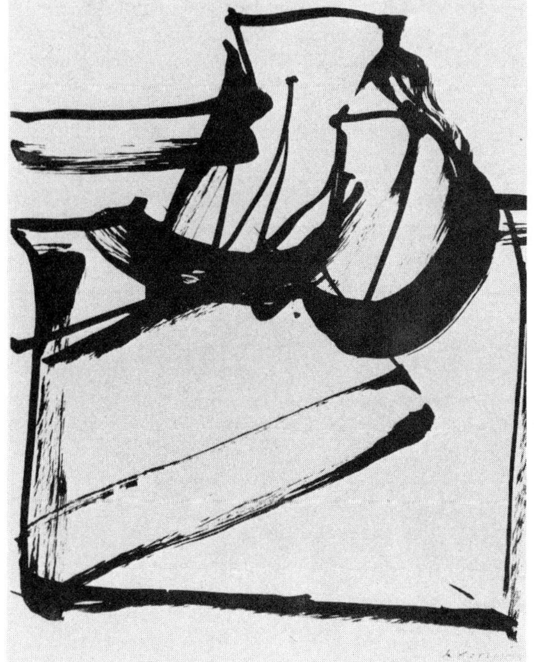

Figure 8-5. We are not allowed to linger in any one area of the drawing. *Folded Shirt on Laundry Paper,* by Willem de Kooning. 1958. Ink, 16⅞″ × 13⅞″. Collection of the artist. (Museum of Modern Art, New York).

in measured relationship to each other. Although there are no identifiable images in the work, we sense the presence of a group of objects. Are they figures? Landscape forms? These suggestions of figurative forms appear and disappear as we examine the work.

If we look at the drawing by de Kooning, we find some of the same sense of suggestion as we do in the Guston (which raises the old question of whether or not it is possible to create a totally nonobjective work), but the de Kooning forms are far more energized than the forms of the Guston. The de Kooning clearly divides the space of the page into chunks of space that form an overall pattern. Our eye, rather than linger suspended in the center of space as it does in the Guston, moves throughout the page—into the corners and out again toward the middle space. The bold movements of the drawing provide tracks, and we are not allowed to linger too long in any one spot along the tracks. We remain conscious of the rectangular form of the page itself and of the highly structured division of the rectangular space.

In both works, the illusion of three-dimensional space exists but is shallow; thus the two-dimensional plane takes on the illusion of a thick slab of space in which the forms interrelate. Both works are poetic; however, the Guston is a soft, lyrical work in contrast to the cutting, stinging quality of the de Kooning. In comparing these two drawings we are not comparing good and bad, or even good and better; we are noting the similarities and differences in related works, each based on a respected aesthetic view. The more knowledge we have of each artist's work, the more at home we feel in the presence of his ideas.

A Picasso drawing compared to a Picasso drawing

It is likely that no artist ever covered so much ground in a lifetime as Picasso. His drawings show us that in the space of a day or two he was able to move through the major ideas of traditional Western art, venture into the forms of other cultures, and still bring off drawings so much his own that they need no identification. Obviously, I could have chosen more disparate works to compare. Instead, I chose two drawings linked to a Cubistic treatment of space but created

Figure 8-6. The reconstruction of space sets the dominant mood. *Study for Standing Nude*, by Pablo Picasso. 1908. Conté crayon, 33″ × 25″. (Museum of Fine Arts, Boston).

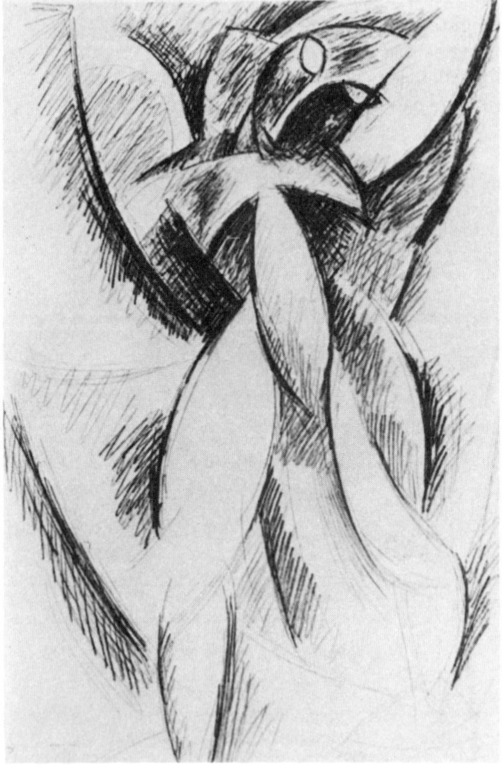

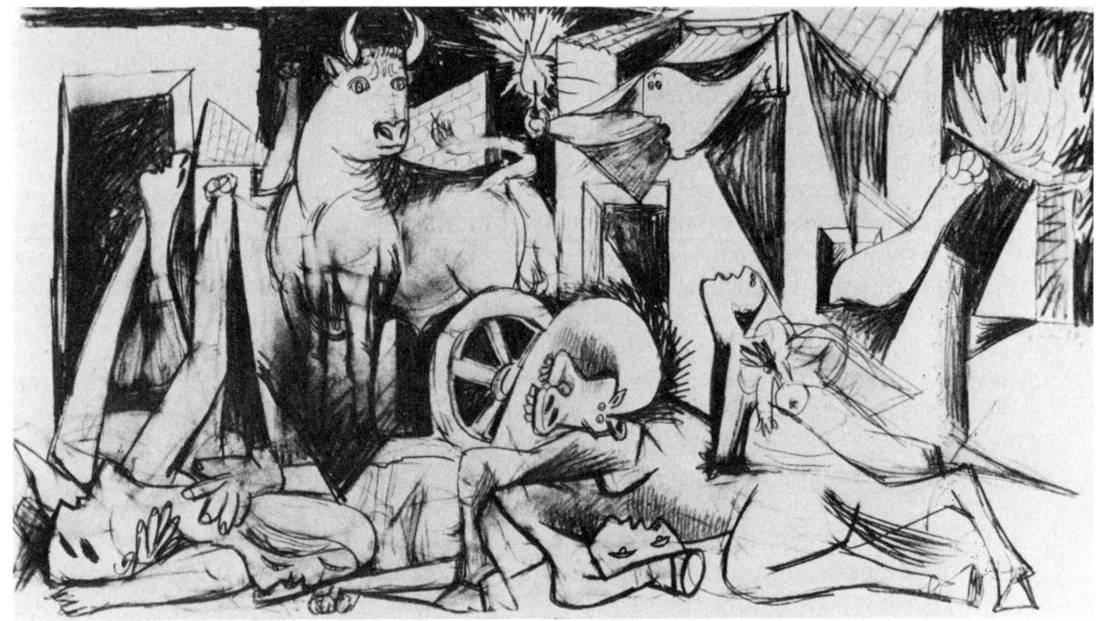

Figure 8-7. Picasso never forgot his priorities as an artist. *Compositional Study for Guernica,* by Pablo Picasso. 1937. Pencil on white paper, 9½″ × 17⅞″. Collection of Museo National del Prado, Madrid. (© SPADEM, Paris/VAGA, New York, 1982).

almost thirty years apart. Each makes use of angular figurative forms, fractured space, and evocations of earlier Western painting. As with the Guston/de Kooning comparison, I do not need to find good or bad—both drawings are respected in the master's body of work. My only task is to point out the intentions in each work and to discuss the methods used to achieve these intentions.

In the *Study for Standing Nude* (Fig. 8-6), Picasso's work is still in its first flowering of Cubism. The human figure has been converted to so many elliptical and ovoid shapes, carving out a space not unlike that found in African sculpture. The implications of the figure's distortion seems to be more for structural than expressionistic ends. There is the slightest echo of the melancholy mood that pervaded his Rose- and Blue-Period figures, but the dominant mood comes from the reconstruction of space he uses to achieve

a dynamism that can be attained only through structure.

The study for *Guernica* (Fig. 8-7) shows Picasso much further along in maturity, and this is reflected in the richness of his expressive means. The ability to dynamically structure space is now a matter of course to be used to strengthen other expressive ends. The reduction of human figures, animals, the inanimate objects, and spaces in the environment to simple geometric forms is more overt than in the first drawing, and the showing of various spatial points of view within one space is more overtly disjunct. The distortion of the faces and bodies is no longer a matter of proving that it can be done, but now provides a means to express the torture and violence resulting from military force—the total disruption and destruction of life on earth brought about by war.

But Picasso never once forgets his

priorities as an artist. The drawing is no mere catharsis. It is a masterfully put together orchestration of straight and curved forces, of positive and negative volumes, of three-dimensional space condensed to fit a two-dimensional plane, of contrasting gestures, and of lines of motion to lead the viewer's eyes to the periphery of the plane but always back into the meaty central substance—the pyramid whose baseline is made up of fallen figures and a fallen horse, and whose apex is the hand-held light in the upper center of the picture.

The movement through space in both drawings is disjunct. Both works show a strong vertical force, but both escape being static through a slight axial tilt as well as a tension in the spatial relationships which pull at the forms, torturing them into a new state of life.

SUMMARY

The critical sense is developed through dialogue; through talking and listening to others talk. When you enter into discussions about art, be candid. Only your honest feelings and opinions are worthy of articulation.

You must also do a lot of looking at art and reading about art. Strive against becoming isolated; you can't depend on the security felt through isolation.

Class critiques with visiting critics are an exciting way to learn about drawing, art, and philosophy, and a terrific place to hear your own ideas examined.

Discussion of quality is always a difficult but beneficial activity. I compare pairs of work as a more pointed way to get at what each work is about than discussing them one at a time would be.

CONCLUSION

Whatever sphere we may be in, there is a profound joy in the realization that we are helping to form the structure of the new world. This is creative courage, however minor or fortuitous our creations may be.

Rollo May

Much of this book has dealt with traditional approaches to drawing. To pass up the wisdom of tradition in a basic study would be a dangerous thing to do. Nevertheless, it is important that we see drawing, even at the beginning, as an open idea without any fixed boundaries in terms of process, form, or materials. The preconception that drawing *can only* be what it has already been is a false and repressive one. In recent years I have seen several new materials enter the market and win favor—felt tip pens and ball points are well-known examples—while others, such as quill pens and bistre ink, are no longer the popular materials they once were. Drawing is now done on enormous scales (Fig. C-1) never dreamed of in the past. Modern drawing has been done with paint, with light, with rope, and with wire. Museum exhibitions and books on drawing do not always reflect these changes, because it is much safer to perpetuate the attitude that "real" drawing can be neither more nor less than it was in the hands and spirits of the old masters. Proponents of this attitude seem to think that drawing was an idea arrived at by nature and revealed to our European and Oriental predecessors in ancient times. I believe that drawing should always try to be more than repetition of historical styles. We who draw or teach drawing should always try to see

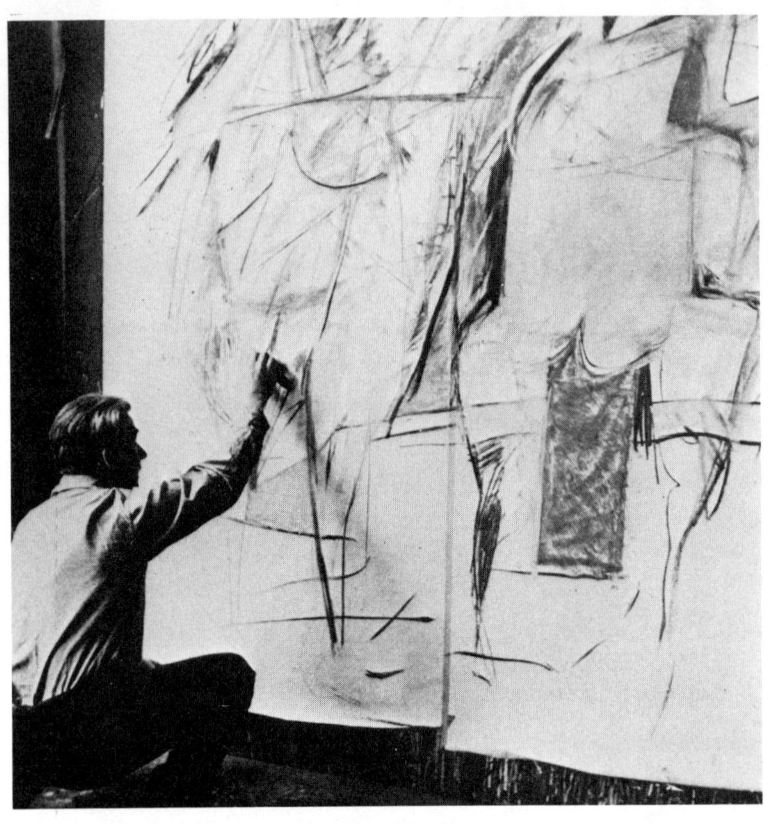

the not-so-obvious possibilities for expanding the medium. Drawing has always been an intellectual and physical discipline free to search while making use of materials that are less permanent and therefore less burdened with object-making responsibilities than oil paint or marble.

The iconoclastic and tumultuous recent history of art has blurred the boundaries that once divided the monolithic media such as painting, sculpture, printmaking, ceramics, and drawing. Historically, drawing refers to the marks on paper made with some of the wet and dry materials described in this book. Recently, drawing has been used as an element in larger concepts, as in the popular film of Picasso "drawing" with a flashlight, or as illustrated by Jim Dine drawing as a part of one of his happenings (Fig. C-2). The *quality* of draftsmanship appears in much of Western painting—sometimes to an advanced degree, as in the paintings of Daumier and the later works of Manet. In these cases paint is used as little more than a complex drawing material. The white canvas is so often allowed to show through, paralleling the role of paper in conventional drawing. All of de Kooning's mature paintings rely on the gestural movement, spontaneity, personal "handwriting," and unfinished surfaces typically associated with drawing.

It is not possible to predict the future of the visual media. Certainly film, architecture, and photography are able to take greater advantage of technology than drawing is likely to do. But as stated in the preface, drawing is not essentially a product-making method but a process, a search which brings the drawer into intimate contact not only with materials but

106

with the physical world being examined. Drawing teaches us to see. Therefore, drawing remains a logical basis for all visual thinking.

This book attempts to increase the availability of drawing in the context that I have described. I make no attempt to show drawing as a "how to" skill. Drawing's unfortunate legacy as a special skill to be undertaken only by the gifted few is an alienating force perpetuated by teachers and artists who have not stopped to examine the absurdity of this myth. The same myth could be true of math and reading.

I have taught drawing in a liberal-arts context for eighteen years, and I am convinced that *anyone* can achieve some level of proficiency in drawing if he or she is willing to make an open-minded effort to learn. After the same eighteen years, I am equally convinced that drawing is as important as math or reading to the full development of beneficial thought patterns in a student. We are victims of cultural habit. Educators at all levels suffer from the simplistic misconception of

drawing as rendering. They are not knowledgeable of its greater potential; therefore they are not able to consider its benefits except as related to an art career. Drawing needs no utilitarian purpose any more than history or geography need utilitarian purposes. A comprehensive course in drawing, philosophically approached and taught by a competent teacher, should be included in everyone's educational experience.

Many books have been important to me during my years as a drawing teacher, but none more important than Kimon Nicolaides' *The Natural Way to Draw*. I, like so many other drawing teachers of my generation, have taken his ideas and reshaped them as necessary to fit our own time and place, as well as my own temperament. Certainly, my greatest hope is that somewhere in this effort of putting together a text I, like Nicolaides, have managed to communicate a fresh idea—however rudimentary—that can be built on by students and teachers who may come in contact with this book.

Figure C-2. Jim Dine in a scene from the happening *Car Crash*. 1960. Reprinted, with permission, from Adrian Henry, *Total Art, Environments, Happenings, and Performance* (Praeger Publishers, New York, 1974). (Robert McElroy).

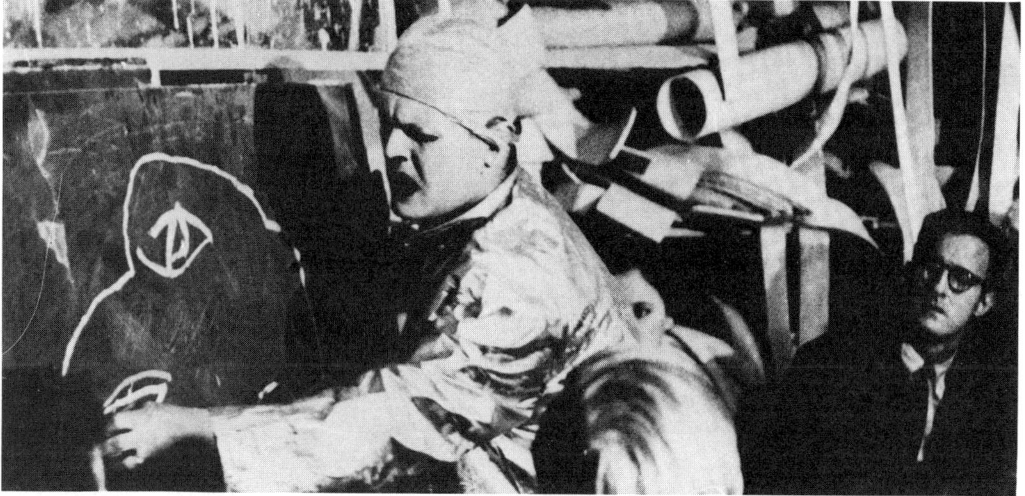

INDEX